W9-CUP-914

Overcoming Arthritis
and
Other Rheumatic Diseases

Overcoming Arthritis
and
Other Rheumatic Diseases

by

Max Warmbrand, N.D., D.O., D.C.

Gramercy Publishing Company
New York

Manufactured in the United States of America

**Library of Congress Cataloging in
Publication Data**

Warmbrand, Max.
   Overcoming arthritis and other rheumatic
diseases.

   Originally published: Old Greenwich, Conn.
: Devin-Adair, c1976.
   1. Rheumatoid arthritis.   2. Rheumatism.
3. Diet in disease.   4. Naturopathy.
I. Title.
RC933.W33   1982   616.7′2206   82-2970
ISBN 0-517-379902   · AACR2

   h   g   f   e   d   c   b   a

INTRODUCTION

by

Joseph L. Kaplowe, M.D.

This book is a product of inspiration. The enthusiastic reports of appreciative patients, once tortured and crippled by arthritis, and now well again, have served as the motivating force behind this book, in which Dr. Warmbrand reveals how he has helped patients to overcome arthritis and other rheumatic diseases. He has achieved these most remarkable attainments through natural methods of healing.

The program of therapy described in these pages is not based on the use of a single, specific remedy; on the contrary, it embraces a new way of life by which there is brought into play the natural healing power inherent in every living organism. This natural tendency to heal can be expressed only when the nutrient elements so necessary to maintain the stream of life are supplied in proper form, and when the patient—taken in hand—is led away from the destructive influences of modern civilized life and is provided with the kind of care that renews his strength and rebuilds his health. The necessary nutrient elements should not be given individually, as fragmentary supplements, but must in the main originate from the products of a good earth; fabricated by the hand of the Great Architect, and wherein are contained all the vital elements, each in proper proportion and in proper relationship to all the others.

In addition to stressing the importance of proper nutrition, Dr. Warmbrand emphasizes the significance of following other basic laws of nature, adherence to which are imperative for healthful living, namely restful sleep, regular planned exercise, the practice of proper breathing and a wholesome optimistic state of mind, all of which play a vital part in the path that leads to a life filled with health and happiness.

Although it is true that the temporary use of a drug may be necessary and useful at times to allay unbearable pain and discomfort, nevertheless, the devastating effect of the long-term use of such substances can outweigh by far the benefit which may be obtained.

In the chapter, Surgery in Arthritis, dealing with hip, knee and other joint replacements, Dr. Warmbrand shows clearly how the breakdown of these joints can be prevented by following faithfully the laws that govern human life and all living organisms. The replacement of a joint, or joints, may, in some instances, give relief from pain and restore function, but ignores the elimination of the cause, or causes, that have brought about the destruction of the joint, and which are, in most instances, the same factors responsible for the breakdown of the body in general.

In this informative book, Dr. Warmbrand guides the arthritic in day-by-day living. By the recognition of natural law, he presents a program for the attainment of health. The book contains—from cover to cover—the rare commodity called "common sense." Those sincerely seeking relief from the suffering of arthritis will not be disappointed, and will spend the rest of their useful lives in gratitude to the man who showed them the way to proper living and ultimate health.

CONTENTS

Contents

Contents

AUTHOR'S FOREWORD

The search for a specific cure for arthritis has gone on through the ages, but at no time has it been as clear as it is now that those who rely on a specific curative remedy are doomed to disappointment.

The world was electrified when the discovery of cortisone was announced. To doctors, this signified the finding of a remedy for a truly stubborn and hopeless disease. To the sufferer from arthritis, it held out the promise that here at last was a cure for this most agonizing ailment.

But cortisone, like all other specific remedies tried before, proved a cruel illusion. What is even worse, its use plays havoc with the health of the patient since it ultimately causes various other destructive changes and increased suffering.

While cortisone turned out to be a failure as a cure, its discovery served a useful purpose; it demonstrated beyond a shadow of a doubt that arthritis is a metabolic disorder. It should be clear, therefore, that if favorable and lasting benefits are to be attained in these cases, all influences that contribute to the derangement of body metabolism must be eliminated, and a program of care that restores normal functioning must be instituted.

The case histories presented prove that arthritis is not a hopeless disease. To obtain results, however, we must return to the teachings of one of the original great masters in medicine—Hippocrates.

Going back to these teachings, we find that Hippocrates enunciated the following three basic laws or principles:

Vis Medicatrix Naturae—We must humbly recognize that no drugs ever cure disease and that only when we work with the forces of the body can lasting results be attained.

Primum Non Nocere—Above All It Must Not Harm! The wisdom of this principle stands out so clearly that it almost blinds us, for how can we ever hope to help the living body unless we employ agents or measures that are congenial to life and that aid in bringing about regeneration and rebuilding of the body cells and systems?

The third principle stressed by this great teacher, but now largely forgotten, is that care at all times must be directed primarily to the whole person, not to the specific disease. We were highly elated to read that Dr. Leonard W. Larson, past president of the American Medical Association, had called attention to these great teachings and pointed out that Hippocrates "fostered the concept of the patient as a whole person, rather than just a conglomeration of many parts." This is what is known in medicine as the Holistic Concept—one that considers man as a functioning whole.

We cannot be too emphatic in emphasizing that only when the specific remedies now employed in the treatment of arthritis are discontinued and we return to the fundamental teachings of Hippocrates, can real and lasting benefits in this disease be expected.

As a youngster I was so ill that no doctor held out any hope for my recovery. I still remember the many times that I had to be rushed to the hospital because of acute fever attacks and the agonizing pains in my joints that accompanied these attacks. On at least one occasion, my fever was so high and my legs so badly swollen that the mere vibration of the floor when somebody walked on it, made me feel as if the skin of my legs were being torn asunder.

The illness was ultimately diagnosed as tuberculosis of the joints. One of the complications that accompanied this illness was the formation of abscesses in different parts of the legs. These abscesses kept draining pus for years, and some of them healed only after my body was able to throw off the sequestrum, the piece of bone that had died off and that kept rotting away. Doctors were certain that I couldn't live long, and that if I did, I would be an invalid.

But then, as an inquiring youngster, I kept reading and finally came to the realization that if I were ever to succeed in regaining health, it would be through a new way of living, a way of living that would provide my body with the care it needed to strengthen and rebuild the health of my bones. I further realized that this could only be done by changing to a carefully regulated dietary program based on the use of food as it comes to us in its natural form, and furthermore, also adopt an otherwise healthful way of living.

This ultimately led to the study of the various healing sciences. In addition to anatomy, physiology, pathology, and other studies related to the structure and functions of the body, I also devoted years of study to the various healing professions such as physiotherapy, naturopathy, osteopathy and chiropractic. The more I studied, the more I came to realize that only when the body is provided with the right kind of food and other healthful care, can it do a thorough job of rebuilding.

Today all that my body has to show for illness of the past are the many scars on both of my legs, reminders of the abscesses that formed when I was so very ill and that kept draining for years. My illness also left me with a stiff left hip, the result of the casts and braces that I had to wear during those years. X-rays of my lungs further reveal the presence of scars which indicate that during the early years, I also suffered from TB of the lungs.

Now, reaching eighty, and in practice for more than fifty years, I am an example of what this healthful way of life has done and what it can do for those who really wish to get well. This book explains how others seriously afflicted and often practically hopeless, who have adopted a similar plan of care, have regained their health. While there are no medicines that can cure arthritis, even the most serious sufferer from this highly debilitating and crippling disease can recover when he or she adopts the type of care advocated in this book.

CHAPTER 1

IS ARTHRITIS REALLY AN INCURABLE DISEASE?

Arthritis is a very painful and crippling disease. It affects millions of people all over the world and makes living for many a nightmare. It is estimated that by now almost 20 million Americans suffer from this agonizing affliction and no country is completely free from it. The statistics listing the number of people who suffer from arthritis do not even begin to tell how many are really affected, since there are millions who, upon examination, disclose deep inroads of the disease, even though they are not yet aware of it because the damage has not yet progressed to the point where it causes pain or shows signs of crippling.

Arthritis, except where it has developed as a result of bodily injury, is usually the outgrowth of a great many debilities or disorders that precede it, or develop in association with it. If the arthritis sufferer is to get well, all these associated disorders must be corrected. The circulation must be restored; the nervous system strengthened; the endocrine secretions regulated. Even when the arthritis results from some accident or physical mishap, the weakened parts of the body must be strengthened and rebuilt and the same essential care is required.

If you have been suffering from this disabling affliction for many years and have tried the various remedies suggested to you, without obtaining any real help, the advice embodied in this book should be most welcome. It will prove to you by facts and case histories, that even the most advanced sufferers from this seemingly hopeless disease need not despair; that in the great majority of cases they *can get well!*

Those who have not yet reached the more advanced stages of arthritis would do well to read this book carefully and make use of its common-sense advice in order to protect themselves against further deterioration and crippling. Those who have already been suffering from the disease for years and who have finally reached the stage where they have lost all hope of ever getting well, will gain renewed courage and faith; they will begin to understand why their past efforts have been unsuccessful and what they must do to obtain the help they need. They will begin to realize that the reason they have failed is not because help in the great majority of cases is unattainable, but because they have not understood how the disease originated, or what they must do to check its further inroads and regain their health.

We are convinced that this new work, with its detailed information and up-to-date facts, will prove a valuable guide to all who are victims of this torturing ailment.

We will start our discussion by presenting the case histories of a few who were as discouraged and as despondent as millions of others, but who, by adopting the program outlined in these pages, and following it consistently, proved to themselves and to all those who knew how sick they were, that with the right kind of care arthritis can be overcome.

We shall begin with the amazing case history of "Helen R.," who for many years suffered from rheumatoid arthritis, a most agonizing and crippling form of this disease. By following the measures outlined in this book, she regained her health.

HOW "HELEN R." REGAINED HER HEALTH

Helen R., then fifty-six years old, had been suffering from arthritis for many years. It started when she was thirty-three years old, and except for certain periods of relief she achieved no permanent results. Her condition had been variously diagnosed as bursitis, lumbago, and neuralgia, but it was not until she suffered a severe attack that she was told she had rheumatoid arthritis. In a report sent to us, Helen describes the agonies that she experienced as "a whole body full of pain."

She flew down to Florida in search of help, but the change of climate did no good. She consulted a doctor who gave her a prescription for metacortone, and the remedy "worked like magic."

"The morning after I took my first dose I was able to get out of bed as if nothing was wrong. For two weeks I swam, danced, stayed up late, walked—and no pain," Helen explained.

The relief continued as long as she continued taking the pills. She went back to her permanent home in Connecticut and everybody was astounded at the change in her. That is, until her pills ran out. "Then I began to stiffen and it was bad. I was very much worse than I had been when I went to the doctor in Miami," Helen continued.

She rushed to a doctor to get another prescription for the same drug and as soon as she started taking it, again, the pain disappeared.

By this time, however, Helen began to realize that the pills did not provide the real help she needed. She discovered that she could not depend on them, for the relief was only temporary. She then decided to gradually reduce the dosage, taking at first four pills a day for one week, then three a day for the week after; taking one pill less each week, until she discontinued them completely.

But this did not work. As soon as she stopped the pills, the pains recurred and she became helpless all over again.

It was at this time that somebody told her that a good diet and a change to better living habits could help. She was told of the excellent results obtained by those who received this care, and since she was anxious to get well, she became greatly interested.

By that time, however, she had become "very stiff and could not walk without help," and arrangements had already been made to send her to a hospital. As a result, her visit to our office was postponed.

After two days in the hospital she realized that she was not given anything that she had not tried before. She decided to leave and return home.

We shall now let Helen continue with her story in her own words. "In a few days my friends helped me out of the house and into a car, and I had my first visit with Dr. Warmbrand. His words still ring in my ears: 'You will be well again, better than in the last ten years.'

"Dr. Warmbrand said that it would not be easy and he was so right. I had promised not to take medication of any kind; no pills whatsoever, and I did not. The pain was severe and many a night I cried, and my nurse let me cry, and finally sleep would come. I was lucky to be just living, and the nurse was very understanding. She saw to it that I was never wakened, because I was unable to concentrate because of pain. I could not chew for three weeks and could not feed myself for the first two weeks after stopping the drug. My hands, feet, knees, became swollen and I needed help to sit up in bed. It was a real job getting me in and out of the hot epsom salts baths twice a day as I could not bend my knees, and my hands were so sore that nothing could touch them.

"If I hadn't been convinced that there was no other way I might have given up. But then, given up to what? So, we kept going, and slowly improvement came. By the end of the third week I knew I was feeling some relief. I welcomed company and began to sit in the wheel chair and watch a TV program. At the end of four weeks I didn't need the nurse and got a housekeeper. She stayed with me for six weeks, and after that my good neighbor came in several times a day to help with preparing vegetables and the bath. It was August 8 that I first saw Dr. Warmbrand and on Thanksgiving Day (how appropriate!) I, without any help, bathed, dressed, got breakfast, took a taxi to the railroad station, walked up two flights of steps to the train, and spent Thanksgiving Day with my family in New York City.

"What a joy being able to care for myself again, and I am still enjoying it. My daughter has since had two more children and each time I stayed with her and cared for the entire family. A pleasure to start the day at five, preparing good foods for the children and mother.

"After a happy Christmas visit with my daughter, I spent the winter at 'Paradise, Florida' (The Florida Spa) in Orlando and there met my present husband. He, too, had recovered from a serious illness, also under the care of Dr. Warmbrand, after having had the same futile experiences I had previously encountered." (Louis R., some time before, suffered from a serious heart condition with various complications. He was under the care of leading specialists but did not seem to progress, and only when he changed to a program in line with the principles discussed in this book did he regain his health). "At the Florida Spa, without taking any drugs, I swam, danced, walked, and had no pain. I enjoyed meeting so many people with the same experience I had. We all had fun together.

"A year later, Louis R. and I were married. We have a travel trailer, and later on we spent four months in Mexico and two months in California. Last year we moved into our own home in New Jersey, next to my mother's. A large yard gives us a 50 by 50 spot for our organic garden. I do most of the work in the garden. This means digging and the ground is like cement, so I must use a pick. I'm up at 5-6 most mornings and I spend the early morning working in the outdoors. This summer I climbed a 36-foot ladder into a cherry tree in my neighbor's yard and picked about 200 lbs. of cherries and froze and canned lots of the apples, too. I am doing all my own housework. My mother says over and over, 'Where does she get the energy?' And I say, 'Mom, I'm happy, I'm eating right. I get a good night's sleep every night, and once in a while I get the chance to help someone as I was helped.'"

In a letter written to us while she was at the Florida Spa,

Helen R. describes how well she felt in the following words: "My heart is filled with gratitude to you and for you this morning and I want to tell you just why.

"Last Sunday at Sanlando Springs, I sat down on a blanket in a way that I haven't used for years, without using my hands. It is the way a ballerina takes a bow, putting one leg backwards and with the back of the toes on the floor, you lower the body slowly until you are sitting on that leg. All without using the arms. I felt so good being able to do that, for it is the way I used to get down on the floor until my legs began their trouble.

"Also, yesterday in the exercise class, I got down on both knees and this morning no ill effects. So, you can understand why I am thinking very beautiful thoughts of you."

Two years later, while traveling with her husband in their trailer, she sent a postcard to us which read as follows: "I'm sure you feel that we have forgotten you, but that is not true. We think and speak of you often. Last week, a woman I met asked me to come to her house and tell my 'story' to a few of her friends who are looking for health. I told them about your wonderful help to me, and that without your advice I would most likely be in a nursing home and helpless or dead by now."

Now, you are likely to say, "but one swallow doesn't make a summer!" We agree, and so we shall have Mrs. S. tell you how she regained her health.

THE CASE OF MILDRED S.

Mildred S. was forty-four years old when rheumatoid arthritis hit her with full force. With it came a terrible loss of weight; the pains were agonizing, and many acutely distressing symptoms began to affect her entire body.

She came to us for care after reading one of our books— *The Encyclopedia of Natural Health*. She realized that none of the medicines prescribed for rheumatoid arthritis offers lasting help; relief is only temporary. The patient recalled what happened to her mother who suffered from the same disease: "My own mother had rheumatoid arthritis over a period of eighteen years before she died, and doctors had little to offer her beyond partial relief of symptoms and pains." (Some doctors believe that a predisposition to rheumatoid arthritis is inherited, but with proper care even with this predisposition, the disease may not develop).

Mildred stated that three doctors consulted about her arthritis had nothing to offer but some of the remedies that relieve pain by suppressing it. She had to travel more than 700 miles to get to our office, but made the trip because she was determined to find out if we could help her.

MILDRED S. SIX MONTHS LATER

Now that you understand what brought Mrs. S. to our office, how did she feel six months after she adopted our type of care? Here is how she describes it in her own words:

"The headaches that have plagued me for over twenty-five years are no more; the blood pressure that once showed a reading of 200/120 is normal; the blood sugar disorder (she was also told that she was suffering from hypoglycemia or low blood sugar) is no longer present. The problem of constipation has improved considerably, and the stiffness and inflammation of the arthritis has nearly vanished."

Mildred and her lawyer husband were elated. Mr. S., who at first was not convinced that our care could help his wife, did not mince words in a letter to us:

"I am very happy to report to you that Mildred has improved tremendously since our last visit to you. I cannot put into words just how much she has improved; you will have to see for yourself."

In a subsequent letter about one month later he again shows how pleased he is when he remarks:

"I am extremely happy to report that this past month has seen a tremendous improvement in Mildred's health. She is able to do more and more things for herself. She was able to go to dinner to celebrate our twenty-first Wedding Anniversary; has been going for a walk daily, and has driven the car for the first time. I am sure you will agree this is certainly some improvement."

Somewhat later Mildred herself wrote to us:

"I have seen many friends and acquaintances with arthritis. I have seen the results of conventional medical treatment, and I have also seen it first hand with the results in my mother's case. I watched her attitude of hopelessness as the doctors kept saying that no one knows the cause or cure. All that could be done was to give relief from symptoms, and still she kept suffering, her life ending confined to a wheelchair. If there is any greater hope for victims from this disease than in the type of care advocated by Dr. Warmbrand, may God guide the medical profession to it. If there is no other type of care that can do it, may God guide the medical profession to him."

SEVERE REACTION PART OF HER RECOVERY

At one time, in Mildred's case, we were faced with a most difficult problem—not because of her arthritis condition, which by then had shown a great deal of improvement—but because of one of the most frightening reactions that we have ever encountered.

From childhood, Mildred had a history of illness and suffering, and among the complications we had to deal with was hypertension (her blood pressure as we pointed out before was 200/120, and she had broken-down kidneys).

While under our care and improving, she suddenly, without any warning, developed a most alarming kidney reaction. Her feet and legs began to fill up with fluid, and her weight, normally no more than 84 pounds, increased daily. She displayed what seemed to be the typical signs of nephrosis: a disease where the filtering glomeruli of the kidneys have broken down to the point where they can no longer prevent the loss of protein from the body. It was this loss of protein that caused her body to swell up.

To make certain we were correct in our assumption that this was only a temporary reaction and not something worse, we suggested that she visit one of our medical associates for a complete work-up. But the report received from him, after a series of laboratory tests and X-rays, was not reassuring. His conclusion was that the malfunctioning of Mildred's kidneys led to the loss of serum albumin, and the associated edema (swelling) was due to a serious disorder of the pancreas—a disorder he considered practically hopeless.

To verify his findings, however, this doctor suggested that the patient be sent to one of the nation's most renowned medical centers, where a noted specialist could examine her.

We were glad and relieved when the report from this specialist arrived; it proved we were right in our assumption: Mildred suffered from an intermediate reaction as part of her condition. With the help of this specialist, it wasn't long before the reaction cleared up. Mildred is now in better health than she has ever been. There is not a sign of any of her former ills, and she is free of all her pains and aches, and is able to do anything she wishes to do, without any difficulty. She is proud of the fact that she has been able to register for college courses at the local college. As she describes it, "It is something I have wanted to do for many years, and it is a very interesting and satisfying dream come true."

UNBELIEVABLY PAINFUL
ARTHRITIS OVERCOME

As further proof that arthritis sufferers need not despair; that recovery is possible when the right care is provided, Mrs. I.'s case should be convincing. She writes:

"Approximately four years ago I was forcibly stricken with some unbelievably painful arthritis in both a shoulder and a knee. I had suffered for years with the nagging pains of arthritis, but this attack was unbearable. Since I'm a business woman, this handicapped me to the danger of losing my position. I could neither pull myself up or step high enough to get on a bus, and taxis became a financial hazard. Previous attacks had all lasted well over a year and I was desperately concerned.

"At this point, a friend of mine told me of the wonderful success he had had with natural treatments. But these treatments were being given by Dr. Warmbrand, whose office was out of town and I was in Manhattan trying to continue my work. Nevertheless, I bravely made arrangements to get a train out of New York at 5:30 p.m., and I did not get back to New York until 9:30 p.m., always in pain—and this twice a week! At first, it seemed impossible to stand the regime; I was over sixty. After one month, during which time the pain grew worse, I finally noticed a lessening and I could get out of bed in the morning without it taking fifteen minutes. Nothing could have persuaded me to stop at this point. However, and alas! a few weeks later, I had a terrible fright. What seemed like a terrific setback occurred. Both legs erupted in a flaming rash and pain again increased to an excruciating degree. Dr. Warmbrand assured me that this was indeed a 'good symptom.' I had never connected symptoms with anything 'good'! At many moments I felt that I was on the wrong track and must back out. However, my faith in my mentor by this time was such that I overcame my fear and replaced it with added determination, courage and trust. Through snowstorms, dampness and miserable winter weather, I continued. By the end of four months I was a different person. Not only had the acute attacks vanished, but also the nagging pains I had known for years were gone.

"Since then, I've traveled to remote parts of the world and have continued my business efforts. It was not a miracle. It was Dr. Warmbrand giving his best knowledge and efforts, and a patient's cooperation to the last notch. Sheer team-work. I shall never in my life go back to old, bad habits which were corrected en route. I never have a pain . . .!"

LET'S HEAR WHAT MRS. F. HAS TO TELL

Why do we give you these stories the way the patients tell them? We could describe their case histories in our own language, the way doctors usually do when they write out their reports, and then go on telling you how they were helped. But who knows better how deep the pains were? Who can describe better than the patient the severe sufferings and agonies? We want to add as a bonus, one more story, and have asked Mrs. F. to tell you how she came to adopt our care and what it has done for her. Here is what she says:

"From earliest childhood I have had very poor health.

"At the age of five I contracted whooping cough, diphtheria and adenitis, which kept me in bed for a period of two years—leaving me seriously anemic, together with a thyroid and glandular disturbance, as well as a bad bronchial and lung condition.

"My father was a diabetic—and I developed a low blood sugar condition. Altogether, I merely endured a miserably weak childhood.

"Upon maturing and entering the business world I functioned on nervous energy only, thus destroying what little 'health' I ever had.

"I lost my tonsils, appendix and developed a gall-bladder condition. At that point, arthritis made inroads in my body. My joints stiffened and enlarged and the pain became nearly unendurable. I made the rounds of doctors, who tried various medicines and treatments—but I grew steadily worse, until it became agony to even attempt to walk. Their verdict was that I had no hope of recovery and should resign myself to the eventual 'wheelchair' state.

"After about ten years of doctors and treatments, I 'by accident' visited a Health Food Store—and I bought a copy of a magazine containing a review of a book by Dr. Max Warmbrand. I read the article and immediately contacted Dr. Warmbrand. Upon examination he agreed to treat my condition.

"I started with his fruit fast—epsom salt baths, and diet of raw salads, fruit and steamed vegetables, and periods of rest, as well as osteopathic adjustments.

"Within a month I experienced the loss of arthritic pain,

as well as a feeling of 'good health' and energy such as I had never before known.

"After about two years of treatment and diet, my gall bladder and gland condition cleared up, and I have nearly normal use of all my limbs and joints. The swellings are gone—and it is good to be alive at last."

Here you have the experiences of four people who were badly crippled and who suffered severely from this disease, but who, by changing to an entirely new approach, proved that *arthritis is not an incurable disease.*

CHAPTER 2

FACTS WORTH KNOWING
ABOUT ARTHRITIS

The question now arises: What care did these sufferers receive that helped them get well?

Before discussing the measures that proved so successful in these cases, let us spend a few minutes in explaining what arthritis is and how it develops.

Arthritis is a form of rheumatism afflicting the joints of the body. It occurs in various forms and is classifed under different names, but the two most outstanding types are rheumatoid or infectious arthritis and osteo or degenerative arthritis. The rheumatoid type is usually found among younger individuals, while the osteo variety usually affects the middle and older age groups. Another essential distinction is that rheumatoid arthritis, especially at its onset and earlier stages, is normally of an inflammatory nature, while in osteoarthritis, certain degenerative changes begin to show up almost from the very beginning.

Other manifestations of the same genre are muscular rheumatism, also known as myositis or fibrositis, and neuritis, which develops when the nerves become painfully inflamed or damaged. The common backache known as lumbago, the severe shoulder pains known as bursitis, the slipped disc or sacroiliac or lumbosacral subluxations, are other related disorders which, if not properly cared for, often blossom into full-grown arthritic conditions.

All these ailments have a common background, and except for those cases which arise because of local injury or strain, are mostly the outgrowth of a general systemic aberration. You will find some of these related complaints discussed more fully in subsequent sections of the book.

A diagnostic evaluation of arthritis sufferers (or those who have allied disorders), usually discloses a variety of other physical derangements. It is well known that glandular troubles predispose and contribute to the development of rheumatic diseases. Poor circulation, nervous afflictions, and various digestive ills, are also often present in these cases. Many patients suffer from constipation and various allergies, while chronic fatigue usually plays a major role.

These associated physical disorders clearly prove that arthritis is not merely a disease of the joints, but part of an over-all breakdown in the functions of the body. The damage in the joints is merely one of the many closely interrelated problems.

ARTHRITIS—A METABOLIC DISORDER

Stating it somewhat differently, in arthritis we deal with a disordered metabolism. This leads to an impairment in the nutrition of the joints; impairs the utilization of calcium, and gives rise to a great many other profound changes in the tissues of the joints. It results in the deposit of excessive amounts of calcium and other minerals in and around the joints, causing them to become thickened and distorted. Alternatively, the bones become depleted of their vital minerals, leading to rarification or porosity, accompanied by various destructive changes as well as an impairment in function. The loss of calcium and other essential minerals tends to make the bones soft and fragile. This condition is known as osteoporosis.

The cartilages (pads which cushion the joints and provide them with flexibility and springiness), become brittle and hard and in time may be completely wasted away. The synovial lining which secretes the lubricating fluid for the joint becomes thickened, impairing the ability to supply the lubrication needed to protect the delicate joint surfaces.

WHY CONVENTIONAL TREATMENTS FAIL

It should be clear from what we stated above that if arthritis victims are to get well, their need is not merely to find a remedy that provides relief from pain, nor is it sufficient merely to treat the joints. The need is to plan a program of care to help overcome all existing disturbances and restore all the organs of the body to normal functioning and health.

That the conventional remedies employed in the treatment of this disease fail in their objective, is by now fully evident. Aspirin, an old standby in the treatment of arthritis or any of the other rheumatic diseases, can always be counted on to provide relief, while codeine or some other similar drug is often prescribed when a change to another pain-relieving remedy is considered advisable. Gold injections are often used in the more difficult cases while cortisone or some of the other related hormones have, in recent years, been regarded as virtual specifics. What is frequently overlooked, however, is that while these remedies often provide relief, they neither correct the metabolic disorder nor do they help to rebuild the patient's general health. They ease pain by suppressing or masking symptoms, but they do not in any way provide any lasting help.

What is of even greater significance is that while these drugs inhibit pain and create a greater degree of comfort for the moment, they most often lead to more damage and, in the long run, contribute to invalidism.

THE FAILURE OF CORTISONE

We cannot forget the time when cortisone was first introduced. As if by magic, arthritis sufferers were made to walk, jump, run, dance. The enthusiasm of these victims of a tragic disease knew no bounds, and doctors, too, exulted, since they thought that the solution to a baffling ailment had at last been discovered.

Today most doctors know how dangerous the drug is, and what is more, nobody can predict the damage which may follow its use. The following, quoted from an editorial published in the *Journal of the American Medical Association* only a few years after the introduction of cortisone, explains how rapidly the disillusionment set in:

"During the 11 years in which naturally occurring and synthetic corticosteroids have been employed in clinical medicine, a gradually increasing list of untoward side-effects have accumulated. Most reactions were recognized and reported in the first two years of clinical experience with these drugs. It was then known that the major or serious effects consisted of peptic ulceration, osteoporosis with spontaneous fractures, mental disturbances including psychoses, and activation or extension of infections. A few years later, necrotizing arteritis, associated in some cases with neuropathy, was added to the list."*

There is not much to be happy about when remedies supposed to help overcome arthritis can cause ulcers, softening of bones with resulting fractures, mental and psychic disturbances, severe infections, destruction of arteries and deterioration of nerves!

"The series of minor effects (much larger than that of major reactions), has also been growing, but only a few have been added in the past five years. It is, therefore, surprising that still another adverse effect now comes to our attention, namely the formation of circumscribed posterior subcapsular cataracts (PSC), as described in this issue of the *Journal.* Seventeen (30 per cent) of 44 corticosteroids-treated patients with rheumatoid arthritis exhibited the lenticular lesion." (Extract from the same editorial).

Hypertension, diabetes and the reactivation of tuberculosis are other serious side-effects which often follow the use

Journal of the American Medical Association, September 10, 1960.

of these drugs. Many doctors have finally come to realize that they can be extremely hazardous.

Drs. Freyberg, Traeger, Squires, Adams and Stevenson, outstanding arthritis specialists, recognized the risks involved when they stated that they "have been disappointed in the post-cortisone events." They noted "relapses in 83 per cent, including those of less than six months duration, even after treatment for as long as a year," and called attention to the "severe withdrawal syndrome," and the "difficult post-cortisone readjustment to the worsened state of arthritis. . . ."

"There is no evidence that the course of the arthritis is ultimately altered favorably by prolonged cortisone therapy as we used it," these authorities continued, and finally made it clear that "whenever cortisone is employed, troublesome effects must be expected in some patients and the physician should be prepared to meet them."*

Dr. Russell L. Cecil, another arthritis specialist, one-time National Director of the Arthritis and Rheumatism Foundation, also called attention to the risks inherent in cortisone therapy when, in an interview with William Kitay, he stated: "Like insulin in diabetes, these two hormones (cortisone and ACTH), must be continually given to maintain the desired benefits. When discontinued, relapses will occur in most cases.

"Unfortunately, a considerable number of arthritis sufferers cannot take these hormones for any length of time without developing unpleasant and sometimes severe side-effects," he emphasized.**

Dr. Floyd S. Daft, Director of the National Institute of Arthritis and Metabolic Disease of the U.S. Public Health Service, explaining why new drugs are being sought for the treatment of arthritis, stated that while cortisone and

---

*Journal of the American Medical Association, December 16, 1961.
**New York Herald Tribune: "The Truth About Arthritis," December 5, 1964.

ACTH offered the best results until last August, they "can cause the body to retain salt and water . . . putting a strain on the heart and kidneys. They can cause a puffing of the face—'moon face'. They can cause unwanted facial hair to grow, particularly in women."*

The damage caused by cortisone and the various other related preparations such as ACTH, prednisone and prednisolone, is incalculable. It leads to a disturbance of sugar metabolism, impairs the utilization of protein, deranges the metabolism of fats and often results in the development of a full or puffed face and also the so-called "buffalo hump."

These drugs cause a retention of sodium and upset the calcium-phosphorus balance in the body; they produce an accumulation of fluid in the system, cause a loss of vital minerals, and often induce a complete breakdown of the body's healing powers.

They damage the blood, the brain, the kidneys, the liver, as well as the other vital organs of the body. We cannot conceive how drugs that have such a disruptive effect can in any way be beneficial to the patient or be depended upon to rebuild real and lasting health.

Cortisone and its related hormones are normally secreted by the adrenal and other glands of the endocrine system. It is now fully recognized that derangement in the functions of these glands contributes to the development of arthritis. That the artificial use of these hormones can step up, or alter, the functions of the endocrine system and provide temporary relief is a well-known fact. However, it should not require much thought to make us realize that unless the functions of these glands are truly rebuilt, the use of such remedies can, at best, give but a brief lift. In the long run, they only create more damage. It is like applying a whip to a tired horse. The horse is made to run faster for a spell, but the point of reckoning cannot be avoided. Collapse is inevitable.

Hans Selye, in his monumental work, *Stress*, recognized

*U.S. News and World Report, June 1, 1955.

rather early that cortisone and its related hormones could have a dangerous effect on the body. In his book, originally published in 1950, Selye points out that the stresses of life cause an increased discharge of corticoids and then propounds the idea that "all the stresses and strains of normal life are met by a similar corticoid production." He reasons logically that this is an aspect of the adaptive mechanism of the body; part of its general defense mechanism. He explains that it was these observations that led to the conclusion that a promising way to treat the stress factor of disease would be to "imitate the counter-shock phenomena, e.g. by administering supplements of ACTH and corticoids when required."

But then he continues:

"Only several years later did it become evident that under certain circumstances, increased endogenous (internal) production during stress, or exogenous (external) administration of ACTH and corticoids can itself become the cause of disease (e.g. hypertension, arteriosclerosis, diabetes, gout, myocarditis and various rheumatic-allergic conditions)."

THE FUTILITY OF OTHER REMEDIES

Turning to aspirin, we wish to point out that, while in recent years cortisone and its other related preparations have been in the limelight, aspirin is still the perennial remedy, and now that the hazards of the cortisone family of drugs are being more fully recognized, this panacea is regaining its old-time importance. Countless sufferers from arthritis and other rheumatic diseases keep taking aspirin for life, and many become so dependent on this drug that they seem no longer to be able to do without it. They must take it before they get out of bed, and cannot carry on any of their daily activities without taking it regularly.

If people would only realize how much damage this commonly-used drug can cause: Graham and Parker, discussing its effects, write: "Sodium salicylate (a salt of aspirin), is widely used in the treatment of acute rheumatic fever and the more chronic forms of rheumatism. While there may be disagreements as to its precise value in the therapy of various rheumatic conditions, there is general agreement that it is a toxic substance giving rise to a variety of untoward and even alarming symptoms which may interfere with its administration."*

Sidney O. Krasnoff and Mitchell Bernstein, describing the toxic effects of the common aspirin, state: "It is evident from the pathologic findings in our case, as well as in the fatal cases with necropsy (autopsy) reported by others, that many of the symptoms and signs of acetylsalicylic acid (aspirin) poisoning are the result of changes chiefly in the brain, kidneys and liver." They continue: "The cerebral changes may resqlt in a chain of symptoms varying from headache, dizziness, vertigo and tinnitus, down to stupor, coma and death."**

News reports released following the tragic experiences with thalidomide contain warnings to pregnant mothers that they should abstain from taking aspirin, since this remedy, too, is known to have caused defective births. The following is by the Associated Press:

"WASHINGTON (AP), Sept. 5, 1975—Women who take aspirin regularly during pregnancy suffer a high rate of complications such as bleeding and infection and endanger their babies, according to a report by two Australian doctors.

"In the Australian study, among 63 daily aspirin users— women who took two to 12 aspirin doses a day—four had stillbirths, compared with none among the babies of 63 comparable nonaspirin-users.

"Among 81 women who took aspirin less often, but at least once a week, there was one stillbirth and three babies died after birth.

---

*Quarterly Journal of Medicine, April, 1948.
**Journal of the American Medical Association: "Acetylsalicylic Acid Poisoning," November 15, 1947.

"The Australian study was published in the Aug. 23 issue of the British medical journal *Lancet*.

"Thirty per cent of the daily aspirin users and 27 per cent of the lesser users had complicated childbirths, such as Caesarean section or breech or forceps deliveries, compared with 11 per cent of nonaspirin users, according to the study."

Aspirin is used because it eases pain and provides a great deal of comfort. However, since the relief is obtained primarily by masking disease symptoms, and since its use can lead to many serious side effects, it should be obvious that if these patients are to obtain real help, this remedy, too, will have to be discontinued and a more fundamental approach adopted.

THE DANGER OF GOLD INJECTIONS

That gold injections are highly toxic is recognized by all. Various skin disorders, stomach and intestinal ills, kidney and liver ailments, headache, dizziness, severe neuritis, deafness, eye impairments, hemorrhages under the skin, ulceration of mouth and gums, general debility and secondary or primary anemia, are some of the complications that often follow its use. In our *Encyclopedia of Natural Health* we call attention to the statement by Dr. William B. Rawls, in which he explains that "although chrysotherapy (gold therapy) has been used in rheumatoid arthritis for eighteen years, there is still a difference of opinion of its real value." Aware of the dangers of this remedy, Dr. Rawls advocates the use of small doses rather than larger ones, but admits that even from small doses, "toxic reactions may result." He warns: "Liver damage may occur and may cause death. Loss of weight and sudden anorexia (loss of appetite) should be considered symptoms of toxicity and possible liver damage even though jaundice may not have developed."

Dr. Rawls further emphasizes that although involvement of the central nervous system does not occur frequently, "deaths from gold encephalitis (inflammation of the brain) have been reported." He also makes it clear that "at present, there is no method for detecting oncoming toxemia and no proven method of treatment."

The *Primer on Rheumatic Diseases* published by the American Rheumatic Foundation to serve as a guide to doctors, confirms Dr. Rawls' findings when it explains that although this remedy has been used for decades it is still controversial. It then reiterates that "there is little evidence of its long term benefit."

Discussing how dangerous the drug can be, it states: "Unfortunately, toxicity is frequent and in a small percentage of cases, serious. Most common are dermatitis and stomatitis. These are readily reversible on stopping the drug, but if the dermatitis is not recognized early it may exfoliate. Other reactions include colitis, renal injury (with proteinuria or microscopic hematuria) and bone marrow depression with aplastic anemia, agranulocytosis and/or thrombocytopenia. These hemopoietic disturbances may be irreversible and fatal; they occur, however, in less than 1 per cent of cases."

LIMITATIONS AND RISKS OF DRUGS NOW WELL KNOWN

We do not wish to belabor the point of drug toxicity, but sufferers from arthritis and its related diseases should realize that drugs prescribed for these ills cannot provide any real help and that their use is accompanied by grave risks. During a recent meeting at the American Medical Association Clinical Convention, a group of noted authorities specializing in the treatment of these diseases, reiterated the warning.

At this meeting, Dr. Joseph Lee Hollander, Professor of Medicine, University of Pennsylvania Hospital, discussing cortisone, warned that "the mere presence of pain, stiffness and swelling of joints is not sufficient to justify the risk of cortisone therapy," and then went on to say:

"In a recent study of 200 patients receiving corticosteroid therapy, it was demonstrated that long-term steroid administration, even though carefully controlled and used in daily doses of less than 15 mg. of prednisolone or the equivalent of one or the other corticosteroid derivatives, was dangerous in that it carried a mortality rate of almost 5 per cent and the chance of serious complications in an additional 15 per cent of the patients."

Dr. William C. Kuzell, Associate Clinical Professor, Stanford University School of Medicine, discussing sulfinpyrazone, a drug used to promote the secretion of uric acid through the kidneys, and phenylbutazone (Butazolidin, Azolid) and oxyphenbutazone, drugs that are used to counteract the inflammatory condition in gout, stated that while these remedies provide symptomatic relief, they do not in any way alter the rheumatoid process.

"The toxic side effects of phenylbutazone and oxyphenbutazone include sodium retention, rash, aggravation of peptic ulcer, nausea, stomatitis, and, rarely, leukopenia and agranulocytosis," he explained, and then continued that "their use is to be avoided when retention of fluid is a hazard and in the presence of peptic ulcer. Periodic blood counts are also advisable during treatment."

Dr. Charley J. Smyth, Associate Professor of Medicine, University of Colorado Medical Center, Denver, discussing indomethacin (indocin), a drug introduced in 1962 for clinical trial in humans, pointed out that side-effects observed following the use of this drug in the arthritic and rheumatic diseases were headache, nausea, heartburn, vertigo and vomiting. Others less frequently observed included drowsiness, mental confusion, depression and a feeling of detachment.

He then stated: "Great caution should be used in administering this drug to patients with a history of peptic ulcer or gastritis and the drug should be discontinued if gastrointestinal bleeding occurs."

Since doctors often use more than one drug at a time, Dr. Hollander warned: "We must be careful not to place patients in double jeopardy. If we use two drugs that might together produce stomach ulcers such as salicylates and phenylbutazone or salicylates and indomethacin we must ask ourselves if the symptomatic improvement is such that it warrants the risk of inducing an ulcer.''

The *Journal of the American Medical Association* explains the predicament in which doctors who use these drugs find themselves, when it quotes Dr. Nathan Zvaifler: ''Added to the unpredictable and varying course of disease is a further complication arising from the nature of the available therapeutic agents: virtually every drug useful in treatment of rheumatoid disease is potentially toxic.''

The *Journal* then goes on to say: ''These toxic effects include gastro-intestinal bleeding from salicylates, renal papillary necrosis from phenacetin, blood dyscrasias and peptic ulcers from phenylbutazone, dermatitis and renal complications from gold salts, retinal damage from the antimalarials, purpura, peptic ulcer and osteoporosis from corticosteroids, and gastrointestinal and cerebral complications from the use of indomethacin.''

Incidentally, the *Primer of Rheumatic Diseases* explains the many serious side-effects that show up from the drugs used in the treatment of the arthritic and rheumatic ills. How doctors can still go on using these drugs after getting all this information is beyond us.

From what we know and hear we are convinced that many doctors are aware that they are on the wrong track. Unfortunately, they don't know how to extricate themselves from these difficulties and so this evil practice is continued, ultimately creating greater damage and more serious breakdown.

The solution, however, is not difficult.

In a letter to *The New York Times** Dr. George A. Sheehan of Red Bank, N.J., dealing with a subject entirely unrelated to what we are discussing in this book, states:''Actually, the principle of health resides in the patient and it is he, with the physician's aid, who must bring it about.'' He adds: ''What it doesn't excuse however, is the *failure of the*

New York Times, November 6, 1966.

medical profession to actively promote this health instead of scurrying around for dramatic drugs and remedies held forth as panaceas" [our italics]. We are convinced that thousands of doctors would agree; the only trouble is, that since most of them do not know how to go about rebuilding the general health or how to restore the over-all metabolism of the body, they do not know how to be of help to the patient.

HISTORY ONLY REPEATS ITSELF

What we see now is merely a repetition of what has been taking place in the past. Throughout the years, many remedies have been offered for arthritis but none of them has proved of lasting value. Vaccines, sulphur drugs, bee venom, histamine, X-ray treatment and a variety of other nostrums have been introduced at one time or another in an effort to obtain results. Practically all of them have been written off as useless.

No wonder so many arthritis sufferers are despondent. Most of them, discouraged by the failure of conventional remedies to provide the help they need, lose all hope of ever getting well. The repeated failures of the past and those of today have finally convinced them that arthritis is an incurable disease.

What most of them don't realize is that their failure to obtain help is not because arthritis—or any of the other rheumatic disorders—is beyond help, but that by continuing to depend on the usual accepted remedies, they neglect to obtain the care they really need. On the other hand, those with the courage to make the changes suggested in this book tell an entirely different story. The case histories presented here, together with the experiences of thousands of others who followed our program and regained their health, conclusively prove that help in the great majority of cases is obtainable when the right kind of care is employed.

Before entering into a discussion of what this care entails, it would be well to explain some of the factors that contribute to disruption of the metabolism of the body, ultimately leading to the onset of these disorders. It should not require much thought to make us realize that the clues are to be found in our way of living. Faulty nutrition, insufficient rest and sleep, lack of proper physical activities, adverse emotional influences, as well as other health-debilitating habits such as smoking, drinking, late hours, abuses of one kind or another, impair the functions of the body and ultimately give rise to these ailments.

It should, therefore, be evident that if those who have fallen prey to these diseases are to get well, their first task is to eliminate all the devitalizing influences which undermined their health and replace them with a program of care that restores normal functioning and brings about the needed correction.

CHAPTER 3

TREAT THE PERSON,
NOT THE DISEASE

Many educators are acquainted with the saying: "Teach the student, not the subject." Something similar must be stressed when we consider the kind of care the arthritis sufferer needs: "Treat the person, not the disease, or its symptoms."

Our task at first must be to get acquainted with the patient.

We want to learn of his habits, his background, his previous treatments; to find out how far the disease has progressed, and the effects of previous care. We further check for other disturbances or weaknesses, for unless these are corrected, the patient will not get well. The ailment itself, as well as the medicines used in its treatment, often lead to further upsets, while a variety of systemic disorders usually precede the onset of arthritis or other rheumatic diseases.

THE QUESTION OF DIAGNOSIS

This brings up the question of diagnosis. Much is made of the need for a correct one. We certainly agree that it is essential to find out what is wrong with a patient, but how often is this actually done? We place a label or labels, a name or names, on a group of symptoms or on the abnormalities we observe. However, what about the infinite number of existing disturbances not seen or recognized? Furthermore, what about the background, the incalculable factors—unseen or seldom fully understood—that have contributed to the disorder? What about the variety of derangements existing in association with the particular disease—seen or unseen? Diagnosis at best gives us only part of the story, and seldom—if ever—evaluates clearly the full picture or its causes. Our aim must be to try to see the picture in its entirety, since our problem is to counteract or correct not merely what is obvious or visible, but also the many unseen or unrecognized factors that may have played a part in the origins of the disease or that exist in connection with it. One of the major problems is to uproot or eliminate, to whatever extent possible, the causes of the disorders. In short, our task is to set in motion a number of changes that will overcome or control not only the recognizable disorder, but also all associated or preceding disturbances, whether recognizable or not. In addition to this, we must also eliminate or modify the influences that have given rise to them. That is why our thoughts must be directed not merely to a particular disease, in this instance labelled arthritis, or some other related disease, but towards the care of the whole person.

To illustrate our point, let us quote from a letter received from a patient some time after her recovery.

"It may seem strange," Mrs. S. writes, "but for so many months I imagined my visits and consultations with you were for the sole purpose of ridding myself of this terrible affliction of arthritis. Yet when talking to a friend the other day about her arthritis ailment, it dawned on me as she recounted the many other physical disorders that plagued her, that for many years I too had these same complaints. I had been so intent on a cure for the rheumatoid arthritis, however, that the disappearance of the other disorders had failed to impress me. How marvelous a revelation to know that your treatment has effected a cure for my entire being, not just a part of me!"

THE ENTIRE FAMILY BENEFITS

Morton, an arthritis victim who came to see us only about six months ago, tells how his family benefited from our care!

"I am grateful to you not only for the great improvement in my arthritic condition, but for the insights you have given me into diet and lifestyle. I attribute to your guidance the present excellent health of my wife and my 21-month-old child. My daughter has known no significant illness in her life and I feel sure that it is due to your advice on nutrition. So, your treatment of me has touched three lives with splendid results."

COMPLICATION IN MR. B.'s CASE

When sixty-five-year-old Maurice J. A. B. came to find out whether we could help him, his major problem was rheumatoid arthritis. But he explained that he was also suffering from colitis—an acute intestinal inflammation—and psoriasis—a skin disorder which sometimes accompanies rheumatoid arthritis and is often difficult to clear up.

We made it clear to Mr. B. that we knew of no specific remedy for arthritis; if he really wanted to get well, he would have to adopt the type of care that would treat not only his arthritis, but also his colitis and psoriasis. His diet would have to be different from the diet usually suggested for patients whose arthritic condition is not complicated by colitis. And since he also suffered from psoriasis, the hot epsom salt baths helpful in the average case of arthritis would not be suitable for him.

SPECIAL NUTRITIONAL PLAN FOR COLITIS

We explained to our patient that the most ideal nutritional plan for an average arthritis case is usually based on the use of an abundance of green and uncooked vegetables and fresh fruits, plus moderate amounts of all-natural whole grains, and small but adequate amounts of easily digestible protein. However, where colitis or any other acute digestive disorder complicates the picture, raw vegetables and fresh fruits may at first have to be eliminated, or used only in very small amounts. Soft, bland, easily digestible and carefully prepared steamed and stewed foods are preferable, while raw vegetables and fresh fruits are introduced later, and only if the colon has healed sufficiently to enable it to handle these foods without difficulty.

IN PSORIASIS—NO BATHS

In discussing psoriasis, we pointed out that although comfortably hot epsom salt baths relieve arthritis distress, in certain types of psoriasis, baths are not advisable because they may interfere with the healing of this obstinate and difficult skin affliction.

The reason for this should be clearly understood. A hot bath often loosens up and washes off the encrustations or scales that cover the sores or lesions; then other scales have to form to cover and protect the raw patches of skin and allow them to heal. As the inflammation clears up, the scales and encrustations ultimately dry up and fall off by themselves. We have seen many psoriasis patients who, when taking off their clothes, kept shedding massive particles of white scales peeling from their skin while the lesions were healing. In some cases the floor where these patients stood while undressing for treatment was practically blanketed by massive amounts of these tiny white flakes. If the inflamed area has not healed entirely, lighter, thinner coverings will often replace the heavier encrustations, or scales. As healing continues, they continue to dry up, and in time the psoriasis clears up.

One must not assume that the condition may not recur. This disorder is the outgrowth of a profound metabolic disorder coupled with certain nutritional deficiencies not as yet clearly understood.

DRUGS IN PSORIASIS

There is a vast literature on the subject of psoriasis, but as yet very little is known about it. None of the remedies recommended in the treatment of this disease has proved of lasting value. In Mr. B.'s case, an eminent dermatologist prescribed a mercury ointment. The patient applied it for many years; then the specialist stated that the only treatments he could suggest would be X-ray treatments in a hospital. Recently one of our associates mentioned that dermatologists are now prescribing methotrexate for psoriasis cases. Methotrexate is a drug being used in the treatment of cancer; it is highly toxic, and so dangerous that the blood of the patient must be checked regularly to make sure that there are no serious blood abnormalities. Many doctors consider the use of methotrexate in psoriasis worse than the disease. They say, "Why use a cannon to kill a gnat?"

Psoriasis sufferers need to adopt an overall healthful nutritional plan and otherwise adhere to a program of living to rebuild the health of the entire body. A well-regulated plan of living plus careful exposure to the natural rays of the sun or an ultraviolet ray lamp can be helpful, and this type of care should be continued until the disorder has cleared up.

Each case, of course, presents its own problem and has to be judged individually. If the skin is acutely or severely inflamed, baths should be avoided. But as the inflammation subsides and the skin heals, baths may be introduced and are often helpful.

MR. B. ONE YEAR LATER

It is now more than a year since Mr. B. came to us for care. He no longer has to avoid raw vegetables and fresh fruits—the kind of food he could not eat at all at first because of his colitis. As time went on his skin showed so much improvement that he was able to start taking baths again. He writes about his progress:

"My colitis, as far as I can determine, has disappeared.

The psoriasis is slowly but surely clearing up. The only discomfort left over from the arthritis is a minor stiffness in my neck which is healing noticeably day by day. I am hale and hearty and experiencing a feeling of well-being I have not felt in the last twenty years."

HOW THESE PATIENTS KEEP CLEAN

Many of our readers may wonder how those who suffer from psoriasis manage to keep clean without taking a bath, but we can assure you that the body of a person who eats the right kind of food and takes good care of himself smells sweet and clean whether or not baths are taken. When the body is internally clean, the outer parts of the body, too, smell sweet and clean.

When the parts of the skin free from psoriasis need washing, soap and water may be applied freely; if a psoriatic area needs cleaning, the use of a mild skin oil is usually best.

DIGESTIVE DISORDERS NOT UNCOMMON IN ARTHRITIS

Mr. B. was only one of many patients who, in addition to arthritis, suffered from difficult digestive problems. In many of these cases, the digestive disorders precede the onset of arthritis, while in others, aspirin or one of the other prescribed remedies often lead to a breakdown or inflammation of some part of the digestive tract. It is known that aspirin as well as other painkillers often cause occult or hidden bleeding and sometimes even profuse hemorrhaging.

Recently we had occasion to see 87-year-old Elsie S. who first consulted us about her arthritis many years ago. At that time she also suffered from what was diagnosed as recurrent ulcers of the stomach. We had to make sure that she avoided the kinds of foods and beverages undesirable in her case because of ulcers.

We started Elsie on soft, bland, stomach-soothing calming foods, but after her ulcer pains disappeared, a well-rounded food plan helped to rebuild her health entirely.

ARTHRITIS AND OSTEOPOROSIS

On and off, for one reason or another, Elsie's stomach problem would recur and on one occasion she was warned that she was developing osteoporosis. In osteoporosis the bones lose essential minerals and become porous and fragile. When this happens they can break or fracture easily. In many cases of hip fracture, the hip bone fractures, not because the person has fallen, but rather the person falls because the hip bone from which essential minerals have been leeched, suddenly collapses.

Whenever Elsie's stomach problem recurred, we urged her to return to the same soothing, calming foods and the care that had helped her originally. Now, at her advanced age, she is a living example of what a healthful way of living can do for all of us.

ARTHRITIS AND ALLERGY

Various allergic disorders often are associated with arthritis. When we talk of allergy, we refer to a condition in which a body has become oversensitized and reacts adversely to environmental pollutants, odors, emanations, or to certain foods. Arthritis sufferers are often afflicted by respiratory ills considered to be of an allergic nature. Certain skin disorders, as well as digestive problems, may be blamed on allergy. Any of these disorders, if present, have to be corrected if the arthritis sufferer is to get well.

OTHER HEALTH PROBLEMS

Many arthritis patients suffer from a deep sense of depression. Although this may accompany any illness, it may be caused by drugs used to mask pain or to block out symptoms of arthritis. Weight can be a problem. Some arthritis sufferers are overweight; some are underweight and either condition requires attention and care.

Arthritis patients may also need dental care. However, it is important to make sure that teeth are not needlessly removed.

ARTHRITIS NOT AN INCURABLE DISEASE

The story of 74-year-old Mildred P. who came to us for help, and who in addition to a severe form of arthritis involving her right hip, knee and ankle, as well as the upper and lower parts of her back, also suffered from a variety of other ills including diabetes, high blood pressure, insomnia, and constipation, is worth telling.

One of the things that we found most remarkable about this 74-year-old lady was that she was able to name all the drugs that she had been kept on through the years while she was being treated for her various ailments. Because none of these drugs helped her, she came to us. About six months after following our recommendations, all her ills, including her arthritis, had practically cleared up.

Since this lady also suffered from diabetes, her blood had to be checked periodically and this was continued for some time even after there were no longer any signs of diabetes. The blood tests usually came back normal, but on a few occasions they revealed an abnormally low white blood count. To check this out, and obtain the opinion of an authority in blood diseases, we asked a well-known New York hematologist to evaluate her condition. Here is what his report stated:

"Your patient, Mrs. P., is a seventy-four-year-old woman who has had rheumatoid arthritis for many years. The patient was treated with aspirin, but for the past several years she has been treated with diet alone. This form of therapy has been quite effective, so much so that the patient is on no medication at this time. Recently she was found to have a low white blood count but was not anemic. The patient feels well otherwise and has no allergies or other significant illness. The patient states that she did have hypertension, but her blood pressure is now normal.

"Physical examination reveals the patient to be a well-developed, well-nourished woman in no distress. She has some evidence of arthritic changes but is otherwise well in appearance. There is no significant lymphadenopathy and no enlargement of the liver. The spleen tip is palpable one fingerbreadth below the left costal margin.

"In view of these findings, I find no evidence of any underlying medical problem of significance to explain her leukopenia (low white blood count). I would therefore suggest that she merely be followed clinically, and if there are any other changes I would be happy to re-evaluate her."

After receiving this report we talked with the specialist by telephone and he simply could not understand how this patient who had been very ill for many years, recovered, especially since arthritis and some of the other ills from which she suffered are considered to be incurable.

We still see this patient occasionally. The abnormally low white blood count existing at the time we sent her to the hematologist has been corrected. It was evidently an aberration due to the readjustments taking place in her body while it was ridding itself of the drugs and some of the other toxins stored in her system through the years.

Six years later, Mildred P. at age 80 reports that her arthritis, her diabetes and all her other health problems are a thing of the past and as of the present time she is feeling as well as she ever did following her recovery.

CHAPTER 4

ESSENTIAL STEPS
TOWARD CORRECTION

TOTAL REBUILDING ESSENTIAL

When we tell an arthritis patient that it takes time to get well, that painkilling drugs must be discontinued, and that a certain amount of pain cannot be avoided, the answer we most often get is, "What difference does it make? I am full of pain anyway. I'll do anything as long as it will get me well."

This is the only sensible way to look at it. If you are suffering from this most debilitating and often deforming disease, what more could you wish than to get well? Many of those who find their way to our care come only after their joints have been greatly damaged; then they realize that their only hope is to buckle down and do what is needed.

How is our program started? First, *all drugs must be discontinued.* This is an important step toward correction. It is essential that we realize from the very start that any drug or remedy that suppresses symptoms of disease such as pain, fever, etc., undermines the recuperative powers of the body, impairing its ability to rebuild itself.

Patients in search of well-being must realize that the pains or other symptoms are nature's attempts to rectify an unhealthy condition, and that they are only hurting themselves when they resort to measures that suppress these efforts of the organism. The aim of patients must be *not merely to obtain relief from pain or gain temporary comfort, but to rebuild the health of the body.*

ALL DRUGS HAZARDOUS

At this point it is essential to emphasize that not only the drugs specifically used in the treatment of arthritis or its associated diseases, but all potent drugs (those that influence or modify disease symptoms), are inherently toxic and must be avoided. People seldom realize that drugs taken in the past, for no matter what ailment, often contribute to the development of this, and other, chronic diseases. Dr. David P. Barr, in a lecture presented at the annual meeting of the American Medical Association, June 8, 1955, discussing the hazards inherent in the use of potent drugs, made this amply clear when he stated that "past use of drugs may be responsible for the late appearance of symptoms or for the development of a chronic disease such as lupus erythematosus or periarteritis."

Dr. Barr continued: "It seems inevitable that with the increasing potency of drugs and the multitude of different reactions caused by single agents that there could be production of syndromes strikingly like those of previously known diseases." He then emphasized that "adverse actions of drugs might be implicated in the pathogenesis (causes) of collagen diseases," (diseases of the bones and connective tissues).

Dr. Jacob M. Leavitt, noted New York gastroenterologist, in some of his unpublished communications, explains that the concept of the collagen diseases (diseases of the bones and connective tissues) deals with many of our chronic and degenerative ailments such as arthritis, lumbago, myositis, neuritis, rheumatic fever, hardening of the arteries, heart trouble, as well as with profound nutritional changes. He stresses the fact that there is a definite interrelationship between these disorders, and emphasizes that a common denominator or an impaired or vitiated metabolism is usually operating in all of them.

It is important to emphasize that not only the drugs specifically used in the treatment of arthritis or its associated diseases, but all potent drugs (those that influence or modify disease symptoms), are inherently toxic and must be avoided. People seldom realize that drugs taken in the past, for no matter what ailment, often contribute to the developing of chronic diseases.

In some cases, especially where drugs have been used over an extensive period of time and the patient has become dependent upon them, withdrawal may at first be more difficult and will have to be instituted gradually. Complete withdrawal, however, is imperative if lasting benefits are to be obtained.

HEALTH AND BODY-BUILDING FOOD

There was a time when the average doctor replying to the question, "Has food anything to do with arthritis?" would answer most emphatically, "No!" There are many doctors who continue to insist that food has nothing to do with arthritis, but there are others who believe that the wrong kind of food may contribute to the onset of this disease, while a change to the right kind of food can make all the difference between recovery or failure to get well.

A WELL-REGULATED NUTRITIONAL PROGRAM

The first step is to change to wholesome natural foods. The diet should at all times include the use of an abundance of fresh vegetables and fruits, and these should, whenever possible, be eaten raw. When used in their uncooked, natural state, they supply not only highly valuable protein and easily digestible starches, but also the essential minerals, vitamins and enzymes. These foods plus small quantities of the more concentrated protein foods* and wholesome natural carbohydrate foods such as potatoes, natural brown rice

---

*Such as lean fish, fowl or any lean meat, lentils, chick-peas or the bland, unprocessed cheeses.

or any of the whole grain cereals, provide a well-rounded, healthful diet. All processed and refined substances such as the denatured cereals, cakes, pastries, spaghetti, sweets, ice cream; all kinds of white flour products, polished white rice and white sugar concoctions, must be excluded. The rich, highly concentrated foods, such as butter, cream, eggs, various fatty cheeses, as well as the fatty meats and fish, should be omitted or used only to a very limited degree.

PLANNING A HEALTHFUL DIET, SENSIBLE EATING HABITS

In planning meals for arthritis patients, various factors must be considered. Weight, habits of eating, hunger, physical activities; work, as well as the general health of the person, play a part in determining diet. This is why it is important for those who can possibly do so, to place themselves under the care of a doctor or practitioner who is fully conversant with sound hygienic principles of health. With experienced guidance these patients will be able to make much more rapid progress.

Those who cannot avail themselves of this help must still realize that only when they adhere to a diet providing all the essential nutrients in their natural and easily-digestible form, will they succeed in obtaining lasting results.

To make sure that an arthritis sufferer derives all the good from his or her food, sensible eating habits must be established. The arthritis sufferer must learn to eat slowly, chew his food thoroughly, eat only when hungry, and make sure not to overeat. The foods eaten should be properly combined—the fewer combinations at a given meal, the better.

SKIPPING MEALS BENEFICIAL

New patients should, if possible, start by abstaining completely from all solid foods for at least one, two or even several days, and should revert periodically to a liquid diet. Restricting food intake to fresh fruit juices, fresh vegetable juices, or the pleasant aromatic herb teas—gently sweetened with honey and flavored with a dash of lemon—rests the digestive system, promotes the elimination of toxins, and prepares the body for more rapid and effective rebuilding.

Some patients ask whether the body on a restricted diet is deprived of essential nutrients. All we can say is that what matters is not how little we eat, but the kinds of food we eat. If we eat only the best of foods, and receive adequate liquid nourishment, a little goes a long way. Remember that a tree grows for thousands of years on one spot, receiving the nutrients it needs during all its life from the soil where it stands. Of course, it also gets nutrients from the atmosphere, but so do we. The tree absorbs the carbon dioxide while we benefit from the oxygen we breathe.

Once in a while we suggest that patients restrict themselves to water, only for a day or two, or even for several days. When this is too difficult, a fruit juice diet, using the juices of freshly-squeezed fruits such as orange, grapefruit, apple, grape or any other wholesome fresh fruit, will do. Sometimes fresh fruits may be used in place of juices, taking one kind of fruit about every two to three hours for one, two or even several days. After this preliminary start, a diet that meets the needs of the individual case should be planned. Those who are overweight or who are not too hungry, may begin by taking one kind of fresh fruit whenever hungry or about every two to three hours during the day. Only one kind of fruit should be eaten at a time. Make a raw vegetable salad the major part of your meal. Then, add to it a moderate portion of protein or one of the easily digestible starches, plus one or two steamed vegetables. This provides a fine meal and supplies all the nutrients needed.

No butter, salt, or any of the other conventional seasonings should be added to the vegetables. We have no objection to the addition of small amounts of soybean oil, sunflower oil, wheat germ oil or freshly squeezed lemon juice and/or the unsalted, dehydrated vegetable powders to enhance the flavor of vegetables—this makes them more pleasurable, especially for those who previously have eaten little of these foods.

For those who feel the need for more substantial fare, the following menu is an example of how a wholesome, natural diet can be planned.

BREAKFAST

Any fresh fruit or berries in season, such as peaches, melons, grapes, apples, pears, raspberries, etc. Those who find this insufficient may add a very ripe banana.

If the above breakfast is inadequate, the following meal should prove more satisfactory:

1. Any fresh fruit or berries in season (from those mentioned above).

2. A small serving of natural brown rice or some natural wholegrain cereal, served with stewed fruit such as stewed peaches, apple sauce, baked apples, or baked or stewed pears. These should be eaten slowly and chewed thoroughly. (Various wholegrain cereals, and natural brown rice, are obtainable at health food stores).

3. A cup of alfalfa tea or any of the other bland herb teas such as camomile, sassafras, linden blossom, etc., slightly sweetened with honey, or one glass of raw, skimmed milk. No sugar should be added to the stewed fruit and when milk is used, it should be sipped slowly or taken with a spoon.

LUNCH

1. A large, raw vegetable salad.

2. Corn on the cob, baked or boiled unpeeled potato, or yams, or sweet potato, or wholewheat toast, with—or without—two steamed vegetables.

3. Baked apple, or stewed or soaked prunes, or any other unsulphured and unpreserved stewed fruit may be used for dessert, if still hungry.

Remember that fruits must be prepared without sweetening, and no salt or butter should be added to the vegetables.

A large, fruit salad composed of fresh fruits and berries in season with 4 to 5 oz. of either cottage, pot, farmer, or ricotta (Italian cottage) cheese, also provides a very satisfactory and wholesome lunch. (The British equivalent is curd or St. Ivel cheese.) We must be careful not to use cream cheese as it is too rich in fat.

DINNER
1. A large, raw vegetable salad.
2. A small portion of your favorite protein food.
3. One or two steamed vegetables.
4. Raw fruits or berries for dessert, if still hungry.

Those who choose the cheese meal mentioned above for lunch, would do well to use baked or boiled unpeeled potatoes or another wholesome starch food, in place of the protein, with their evening meal.

The soft, bland cheeses, lentils, the young, green (cooked) soy beans, or garbanzo beans, provide valuable protein but should be used in moderation. Almonds, sunflower seeds and pumpkin seeds, are other fine sources of protein, and may be used in small amounts in place of the protein foods suggested above. Those who cannot do without meat or fish may use small portions of lean fish or poultry or any lean meat, in place of the other protein foods, about two or three times a week. These foods may be served broiled or baked, but never fried.

The above illustrates the sort of diet that can be planned for those who suffer from these distressing ailments. The meals may be varied to suit individual taste, but should always be composed primarily of wholesome natural ingredients.

MAKE THE SALAD YOUR MAIN DISH
At this point we wish to reiterate that *uncooked natural foods provide the best and most valuable nourishment for the body.* Unless contra-indicated because of certain digestive difficulties, raw vegetable salads should make up the major part of the meals, while the foods that are not eaten

raw should be prepared only in the simplest way possible. Steaming or baking is best and, to repeat.

OTHER FOOD FACTS WORTH REMEMBERING

Bread, cereals and other grain foods should be used only very sparingly or not at all. Potatoes, carrots, beets and parsnips provide easily-digestible starches and are to be greatly preferred. Potatoes should be baked or boiled in their skins and eaten without any butter or salt.

The use of fats must be strictly controlled. Cold-pressed natural oils such as soybean, safflower, wheat germ, or corn may be used in small amounts on the raw vegetable salad to enhance its flavor. *No fats should be used in cooking and again, no fried foods!*

Eggs contain valuable protein. However, they are rich in fat and contain a high amount of cholesterol. For these reasons they are best omitted from the diet. Other foods with a high cholesterol content are butter, cream, milk, fatty meats and the fatty cheeses. This includes practically all types of cheese, except Italian ricotta, cottage cheese (pot cheese), farmer cheese, or the unprocessed goat cheeses.

It should be obvious that the many refined sugars and sweets such as ice cream, candies, cakes, pastries, must be completely omitted. Even the highly concentrated natural sweet foods, e.g., figs, dates, raisins and honey, must be used very sparingly or not at all. Patients should obtain their sugar from fresh fruits: apples, pears, grapes, melons, as well as from the root vegetables: carrots, beets, parsnips, potatoes, yams, etc. Concentrated sugars, even those taken in natural form, lead to excessive fermentation and overstimulation and are not recommended.

Coffee and tea have to be eliminated. Alfalfa, alfa-mint, or any of the other herb teas may be substituted for coffee or regular tea and make fine beverages. A cup of hot vegetable broth made at home out of fresh vegetables, or prepared by adding one heaping teaspoonful of your favorite vegetable broth powder to a cup of boiling water, provides a desirable hot drink. Vegetable juice combinations—carrot and celery; carrot, celery and apple; carrot, cabbage and apple; carrot, celery and parsley—also provide excellent liquid vegetable nourishment. These juices should not be taken in too great quantities; not more than 6 to 8 oz. at any one time. Other beneficial mixtures of vegetables may be used.

A "juicer," or machine for extracting fresh, raw vegetable juices, and a blender are valuable additions to the home. These machines, together with a great variety of vegetable broth powders and tasty herb teas, are available at all good health food stores.

Steamed vegetables are delectable even when prepared without any seasonings, but those who have been accustomed to spices and condiments sometimes find these foods too bland at first. The addition of onion, garlic, dill, sage, assorted herb flavorings, or the vegetable broth powder will improve their flavor.

All irritating spices and condiments such as salt, pepper, mustard, vinegar, etc., and stimulants such as coffee and tea should be avoided. Alcohol is a depressant and must be eliminated. There are many ways of preparing enjoyable, tasty meals without resorting to irritating, health-damaging substances, and the dishes presented in the Appendix should prove tempting.

UNCOOKED, NATURAL FOODS SUPREME

The reason we insist that liberal amounts of uncooked, natural foods should be used whenever possible, is because cooking destroys many of the vital elements and deprives patients of essential nourishment. Natural ingredients, uncooked and unprocessed, provide most valuable proteins, the finest carbohydrates, and vital protective elements such as minerals, vitamins, enzymes, co-enzymes, and the very valuable trace elements.

It is evident that these protective elements are essential to the rebuilding of health. But what is frequently overlooked is that they must be obtained in whole form from living, natural foods, not from artificial or synthetic sources, nor in an isolated or fragmented form. We cannot stress too strongly the fact that *only when these vital elements are obtained from whole, natural foods, can they be of real and lasting value to us.*

In planning the diet, a certain amount of latitude is permitted. We mentioned before that it is best to start the dietary program with a few days on water or fruit juices, or fruit only. In some cases, however, it is often easier to start with a fuller dietary program and resort to a more restricted diet, or fast, later, after the body has been given a chance to adjust itself to this new life style.

NATURAL VITAMINS AND YOUR HEALTH

The question of food supplements and the role they play in rebuilding health is often hotly debated. It is necessary to examine this question in its true light. First, we must understand that food supplements derived from the natural sources in their whole form, containing only basic nutritional elements required for complete body nourishment, cannot be placed in the same category as drugs taken for the purpose of suppressing or modifyng certain disease symptoms. Today, we all know that vitamins, minerals, enzymes and other basic food elements are essential for the preservation of health and the promotion of healing and repair.

We cannot stress too strongly the fact that *nothing can take the place of a well-balanced nutritional program.* Every conscientious doctor and health advocate subscribes to this fact. While this is the only way to obtain all the nutrients we need in easily digestible form, planning it is not always as easy as it sounds. Many things have happened to make the selection of good, wholesome food more difficult to obtain. A well-informed segment of our population long ago began to realize that because of our forced agriculture and artificial farming methods, even foods used in their natural state do not always provide all the nourishment we need. The constantly increasing use of poison sprays and chemicals only damages our produce still further and, at times, can endanger our lives. The practice of picking many of our fruits and vegetables and shipping them to the market when still in an unripened, or only partly ripened state, adds further to the existing bleak picture. With all these man-created deficiencies it should be readily apparent that if we are to receive our full share of nature's goodness, vitamins, minerals, enzymes, co-enzymes, trace elements, proteins, etc., our diet must be planned with care.

Even if all our people were cognizant of the many artificial and harmful procedures employed in present-day agriculture and commercial food manufacturing, only a small number could turn to organically-grown and properly-raised produce, because a fraction of this is available for general use—not enough to supply more than a pitifully inadequate number of people.

Also, there are a great many people who—because of habit or inclination—are unwilling to give up conventional eating habits and adopt a more completely regulated and healthful diet.

Under these circumstances, it seems to us that those who are in search of renewed health and well-being would derive infinitely more benefit if, instead of placing their faith in injections, potions, or medicines, they turned to natural food substances to obtain their required nutrients.

At this point it would be well to define the difference between the vitamins and other food supplements derived from natural sources and those produced synthetically from coal tar products or other chemicals. While chemically they may appear alike, nutritionally they are very different. The natural vitamins and food supplements derived from plants and other natural sources, especially when obtained in complete and unprocessed form, provide vital substances essential to life; those that are synthetically manufactured are mere chemical substances and can scarcely be regarded as foods.

We must realize that natural foods provide not only a wide variety of vitamins and minerals, but also many other vital constituents such as enzymes, co-enzymes, trace elements, protein, and undoubtedly many more that have not yet been identified. All these are necessary for sound nutrition and have to complement each other if real and lasting benefits are to be achieved. Synthetic vitamins—even those in multiple formulae—are devoid of these associated nutrients and while, like drugs, they sometimes seemingly provide a temporary lift, they cannot be depended upon for permanent results. If used indiscriminately, they can even contribute to an upset in the body chemistry. *We have pointed out on many occasions that a deficiency of one vitamin or mineral presupposes a deficiency of other vitamins, minerals and associated nutritional factors. To repair existing deficiencies or protect ourselves against them, all food elements must be obtained in proper balance from natural sources.*

Balance is the *sine qua non* of a sound program of living.

CONTROLLED EXPERIMENTS PROVE NEED FOR PROTECTIVE ELEMENTS

In thousands of controlled experiments the benefits derived from the use of vitamins, minerals and enzymes have been clearly demonstrated. Many noted authorities stress the fact that sufferers from arthritis and other related diseases are deficient in vitamins A, B and C, as well as lacking many of the other vitamins known to science.

But this in reality does not present the whole picture, since a thorough evaluation of these cases would disclose that victims of these diseases suffer from a variety of other nutritional shortages, e.g., minerals, proteins—and possibly trace elements.

This lack in sufferers from arthritis or any of the other allied diseases results from the use of refined and processed foods, or produce that is raised on poor or highly depleted soil, as well as from a derangement in body metabolism.

It should, therefore, be clear that these shortcomings cannot be completely or permanently made good except when we make certain to supply the body with all its nutritional needs from natural sources and follow a program that helps to rebuild normal body functioning. This enables the body to utilize its food in the most efficient manner.

We must never forget that processed and refined foods have been robbed of many of nature's vital elements, while wholesome, natural ones—especially those obtained from whole, uncooked ingredients—provide not only an abundance of all the valuable protective food elements, but also protein of highest quality (although in small amounts), and easily digested starches.

Those who, for one reason or another, cannot make adequate use of uncooked foods, must still make certain to obtain maximum nutritional value from what they eat, and must therefore be careful to prepare their meals so that only a minimum amount of the valuable nutrients are lost or destroyed. Foods not eaten raw should be steamed under a low flame, baked, or prepared in a pressure cooker. We do not recommend cooking with aluminum pots and pans. Stainless steel, agate ware, iron pots and glassware or pyrex should be used.

Furthermore, in the interest of "nutritional insurance," the diet of these patients should be supplemented with freshly extracted raw fruit and vegetable juices.

MORE NUTRITIOUS FOODS NEEDED

Sufferers from arthritis or its allied ills are asked to give up many foods to which they have become accustomed, but this does not mean that they cannot have a varied diet or plan meals that are enjoyable. The essential point is that they must use only those foods that provide real nourishment.

In choosing their fruits and vegetables, they must make certain to obtain the best of those that are seasonably most available, while at health food stores they can obtain a variety of natural, unadulterated and unprocessed ingredients that have not been tampered with by modern manufacturing methods. The unfermented, unsweetened fruit and vegetable juices, the fine, aromatic herb teas, the vegetable broth powders, the varied whole grain products, organically grown brown rice, the unprocessed and unpreserved packaged dry fruits, the various natural oils with their valuable, unsaturated fatty acids such as soybean, safflower, and wheat germ oil—different varieties of honey, the various nuts and seeds, and a great many other wholesome foods too numerous to mention are all available. These provide contrast and make the meals interesting and appetizing.

We are interested in many things that make life meaningful and interesting, and it is about time that knowledge on how to plan a regimen that can protect us against needless disease and suffering should become one of them. Those who acquire this knowledge while still well are indeed fortunate, since they will know how they can remain in good condition. On the other hand, those who are already in need of help will gain a better understanding of how they must go about rebuilding their health, and will know how to work toward this goal.

In writing about the provender available in the health food stores, we do not mean to imply that all that is sold in these stores can be used indiscriminately. The specific needs of an individual patient must always be considered, and selection and combinations are points that must never be overlooked. What we wish to make clear, however, is that those who adopt this wholesome, natural regimen need not feel that they are being deprived in any way, since the foods we recommend are not only beneficial but also highly satisfying.

We wish to reiterate that these foods must not be regarded as possessing specific curative properties. We cannot stress too often that *all healing originates from within the body, and that no foods or drugs have the power to cure.* We recommend this regimen because if the health of the body is to be rebuilt it is essential that the patient be provided, not only with good care, but also with the kind of food that supplies all the nutritional elements needed for renewal.

WHAT ABOUT THE CITRUS FRUITS?

While in the past the citrus fruits—oranges, lemons and grapefruit—have been highly regarded, some are now beginning to question their value. It seems to us that the difficulties observed in recent years in connection with their use have arisen, not because they are harmful, but due to a variety of other factors.

Some cannot tolerate the citrus fruits because, when not fully ripened, they contain a high amount of acid.

Sufferers from arthritis and/or any of the allied rheumatic disorders may be afflicted by a number of other derangements, such as highly sensitive or inflamed nerves, or certain digestive problems. This may make the use of citrus fruits undesirable, even when they are used in their fully-ripened state, but especially when they have not been given a chance to ripen fully before they are picked.

The fully tree-ripened citrus fruits, especially the grapefruit, can be used to great advantage in many cases of arthritis. Patients may be placed on a fruit juice diet for a day or two, or even several days at a time, and the grapefruit juice is often selected for this purpose. If citrus fruits have to be omitted, apple, unsweetened grape, or other fruit juices, extracted with the juicing machine in your own home or obtained from a health food store, can be of great value.

One of the old-fashioned remedies for relieving arthritis has been what has come to be known as the "lemon cure." In this regimen, the patient takes the juice of one-half lemon three times a day, but gradually increases the quantity until he takes the juice of six to eight lemons a day. The process is then reversed. The quantity of juice taken daily is gradually decreased until no more than the juice of half a lemon is again taken, three times a day. This program repeated at certain intervals has proved helpful in many cases. It should be evident, however, that this does not take the place of a carefully planned diet, nor can it replace the over-all program suggested in this book. Vitamin C, as well as the many other valuable food elements in the lemon juice, undoubtedly exerts a beneficial effect on the body. Since the citrus fruit juices (especially when taken in large quantities), are known to have a corrosive effect on the teeth, it is well that they be taken through a straw or not kept long in the mouth. After taking the juice it may be advisable to rinse the mouth with plain water.

If you are not certain whether citrus fruits are advisable in your case, it is best that you omit them. Those who abstain from them need not feel deprived, since they have the choice of a great many other valuable fruits.

CHAPTER 5

OTHER ESSENTIAL
ARTHRITIS CARE

Since arthritis and/or other forms of rheumatism have a greatly debilitating effect on the body, one of the most essential needs for those suffering from these diseases is an abundance of rest and sleep. A nap after the noon meal and rest periods whenever tired or fatigued are highly recommended.

Those who suffer from extreme debility may need complete bed rest for a period of time. Where this is impractical or impossible, they should make sure to take naps after meals, and otherwise as often as possible.

CORRECTIVE EXERCISES DO MUCH TO HELP

A program of corrective physical exercises and other carefully regulated activities, plays a vital part in the rebuilding of the health of these patients. It is imperative that all physical activities be carefully planned to make certain that the body is not overtaxed. Our aim is to strengthen and rebuild the body, and only exercises adjusted to the needs of the individual case can be of real value. Deep breathing exercises should be included in such a program.

BALANCE BETWEEN PHYSICAL EXERCISE AND REST

At this point, it is well to stress that both rest and physical activity must be carefully regulated to provide the care needed. During an acute reaction or when the pains in the joints are most severe, rest, not exercises, may be the primary need. Physical exercises should be started gradually, after the acute pains have subsided or have greatly diminished, and should be gradually increased as the patient's strength returns.

HOT BATHS HELPFUL

Comfortably hot baths with one or two glassfuls of epsom salt or sea salt added to the water, are of great help in these cases. The baths should at first be taken daily, but as improvement is noticed, could be reduced to one every second day. Such baths are usually relaxing and often induce sound sleep. They are best taken before retiring for the night. To maintain the water at an even temperature some of the hot water should be kept running while the patient is submerged in the bath. Afterwards, the patient should don a robe without drying, and then retire and be well covered. This often induces perspiration and is very helpful, since it promotes the elimination of toxins through the skin. If the hot bath proves too stimulating and interferes with sleep it should be taken in the morning or during the day, but should always be followed by a rest period lasting for at least a half to one full hour.

THE APPLICATION OF HEAT

The application of heat to the acutely painful joints often does much to relieve pain. An electric pad or a hot water bottle, or a heating or baking lamp applied to the aching joints, helps in most cases. Occasionally, moist, hot compresses will prove more beneficial. Steaming the afflicted joint is often recommended in obstinate instances. This is accomplished by placing a hot, moist towel over the inflamed and painful area, and then applying a heating or baking lamp over it. This can be done for about thirty minutes at a time, and may be repeated several times a day.

COLD WATER BATHING MUST BE AVOIDED

Cold baths or cold applications usually cause more pain in the arthritic joints and therefore should be avoided. There is, however, one exception to this rule. Where the application of heat or hot baths causes more intense pain, the application of cold moist compresses following the hot bath, or the application of heat, often provides great relief. Hot treatments applied to arthritic or rheumatic joints provide relief in most cases but could be bothersome when the nerves are severely inflamed. Where cold, moist compresses are used, they should be well covered with a dry flannel or a turkish towel, since they must become warm to be of real benefit.

THE NEED FOR EMOTIONAL CONTROL

The need for emotional control and peace of mind as a means of conquering this disease must never be overlooked. Stress, tension, worry, all kinds of emotional upsets are health-destroying and therefore actually interfere with recovery.

Some scientists and researchers actually blame certain forms of arthritis solely or primarily on tension, and while this in most cases is a gross oversimplification, it is well to bear in mind that unless the sufferer makes an effort to develop a more serene and peaceful outlook on life, he will fail in his effort to get well and with time will only continue to get worse.

Patients do not like being told to give up their peeves or resentments. Their excuse is that you cannot change human nature. But this is not true. A healthful way of living, plus right thinking, can do much to make us develop a different outlook on life, and this is wonderful for all of us.

Get help if necessary. Some obtain help when they turn to yoga. Others benefit from group therapy. Some practice transcendental meditation or some other form of meditation, while others may have to seek help from a physician skilled in the handling of these cases. But make sure that the help you get is from a doctor or practitioner who is fully conversant with the principles outlined in this book. Remember, however, that in the long run, it is up to you. Think constructively. Recognize the benefits that you can derive from a more serene and contented outlook on life, and you will never be sorry for it.

THE NEED TO MAINTAIN NORMAL BOWEL FUNCTIONING

Many patients suffer from constipation. Most people are under the impression that one evacuation a day is normal, but this is often not the case. Anybody who eats two or three meals a day should have at least two or three evacuations daily. To relieve constipation, enemas may be used, at first once a day, later once every second day, then at less frequent intervals, until bowel functioning has been restored to normal. Once this is accomplished, the enemas are discontinued.

One of the best ways to encourage regularity is to establish a routine of trying to move the bowels three times a day—morning, noon and night, usually after meals. The patient must be careful not to strain, since this actually interferes with bringing about an evacuation. Results are more likely to come when the patient is completely relaxed. Give yourself at least ten to twelve minutes, and do not worry if results do not come immediately. While it often takes time to rebuild the functioning of the colon, this type of training, added to the other required care, ultimately produces excellent results. Also, the need for obeying nature's call must never be overlooked.

FEET MUST BE KEPT WARM

In arthritis and its other related disorders, one of the major problems is poor circulation. Hands and feet are often cold and clammy. Patients often suffer from cold feet even in very hot weather. To keep their feet at a comfortable temperature is, therefore, a "must"! Warm socks, and the application of a hot water bottle or an electric pad to the feet, are helpful for this purpose.

SUNBATHING BENEFICIAL

Sunbathing, judiciously employed, is of great value. During the hot summer months, sunbaths should be taken early forenoon or late afternoon, when the sun is not too hot. Start with a few minutes exposure on each side and then gradually increase the duration, until a full hour is taken at a time.

HEALTH-DEBILITATING INFLUENCES MUST BE ELIMINATED

Our aim is to eliminate all the influences that interfere with the rebuilding of health. Smoking, drinking, insufficient rest and sleep, late hours, wrong eating habits, overexertion, nervous tension, are debilitating and must be avoided. The wise healer can encourage these changes by pointing out how essential it is that they be avoided. Those who are unable to obtain adequate professional care, and who have to rely on themselves, must realize that nothing is more important than revitalizing the body, and that the minor sacrifices they are asked to make are but a small price to pay for the benefits they will ultimately derive.

THE ROLE OF PHYSIOTHERAPY

Mild, nonstimulating physiotherapy treatments, and careful manipulative procedures, can often be helpful to arthritis victims. Visits to the good spas or bathing resorts, when this can be arranged, also often provide a great deal of comfort and relief.

It is essential to stress, however, that a complete change in the patient's living habits and sound hygienic care are imperative if lasting results are to be obtained.

CHAPTER 6

GETTING RELIEF
THE SAFE WAY

We never minimize the need for relief from arthritis pain but insist that relief be obtained without drugs that mask the symptoms of the disease, because these drugs often produce serious side-effects.

There are safer ways to relieve the severe discomfort of arthritis: various manipulative treatments such as osteopathy, chiropractic, reflexology; the use of hot paraffin baths; treatments by acupuncture or bee venom. We shall try to give you our thoughts on these measures.

OSTEOPATHY, CHIROPRACTIC, OTHER MANIPULATIVE MEASURES

We stress the benefits that are derived from chiropractic, osteopathy, and the various other manipulative measures in the treatment of arthritis, and know from personal experience that when skillfully applied these treatments are usually beneficial. They help to loosen up tense muscles and improve the circulation to the broken down or weakened ligaments and joints.

JOINTS NEED LOOSENING UP

Stiffened or badly locked joints need loosening up. In some of these cases the accumulation of calcium in the joints and/or the development of scar tissue may cause so much stiffness that it may appear as if they could never move freely again. Yet with proper care, the excess calcium is often dissolved and eliminated, while a well-regulated plan of exercises and skillful manipulations gradually stretch or loosen up existing adhesions and/or scar tissue. This ultimately restores flexibility and freedom of motion and sometimes promotes total correction. The only time a joint can no longer be unlocked is when it has become permanently fused or ankylosed—a condition found in some of the more advanced cases of arthritis. This is also the condition that we find in the advanced type of ankylosing spondylitis (Marie-Strümpell).

SKILL AND CARE NEEDED

Acutely inflamed joints should never be forcibly exercised or manipulated. Make sure to get rid of the inflammation first; then start with gentle, carefully-planned exercises and/or manipulations. *Do everything slowly, gently.* The movements should be gradually extended, never forced. while providing relief they most often also speed up recovery. However, never make the mistake of thinking that these treatments can take the place of the overall healthful plan of living that is required to promote detoxification and general rebuilding.

THE HOT PARAFFIN BATH

The hot paraffin bath provides a certain amount of relief, but that is all you can expect from it. Here is how a hot paraffin bath is prepared. Take three pounds of paraffin to one pound of vaseline. Melt in double boiler but be sure to keep the paraffin away from the open flame. Let the mixture cool until a thin white coating forms on top. Then dip your painful hand in the cooling paraffin but remove immediately. After the fine film of paraffin has become congealed, repeat the dipping five times. While dipping, do not move the fingers. The film of paraffin that forms on the hand feels like a thick glove. This paraffin coating should remain on the hand for thirty minutes and can then be peeled off as you peel off a glove. The paraffin can then be used again and again.

For joints that cannot be dipped into the melted paraffin an ordinary brush can be used to apply it. Make sure that you use the brush several times to form several layers.

ACUPUNCTURE

More recently, acupuncture has been receiving attention as one of the treatments for arthritis.

An authority in acupuncture whom we hold in high regard explained to us that acupuncture influences the body beneficially because of its special effect on the neuro-muscular and endocrine systems (the nerves, the muscles, and the glands of internal secretion).

But this does not say very much since everything we do influences the neuromuscular and endocrine systems. The question is how permanent are its effects. Some of our patients who have tried this therapy reported that they benefited from it, while others were greatly disillusioned. None, however, seemed to have obtained any lasting benefits.

This is very much in line with the findings of a study conducted by Drs. Peter Kyhee, Thorkild W. Andersen, Jerome H. Modell, and Segundina A. Saga of the Department of Anesthesiology, University of Florida College of Medicine and the Veteran's Administration, Gainesville, Florida. The report of this study covering 261 patients with chronic pain on whom 979 acupuncture treatments were performed pointed out that while at first 54 per cent of those receiving the treatments obtained great relief; four weeks later "only 18 per cent of patients still reported an excellent degree of relief."*

When acupuncture first made the headlines, Dr. John J.

* "Treatment of Chronic Pain with Acupuncture," *Journal of the American Medical Association*, June 16, 1975.

OVERCOMING ARTHRITIS ◆ 62

Bonice, chairman of the Ad Hoc Committee on acupuncture of the National Institute of Health, also of the American Society of Anesthesiologists, made a thorough study of the subject, and then reported back that the advantage of this therapy is in its safety—it does not have any of the side-effects of drugs. But then he emphasized that while it is employed as a form of anesthesia in certain cases of surgery, its major benefits are derived from its analgesic or pain-relieving effect.*

We do not as a rule object to the use of acupuncture because it does not have any of the dangerous side-effects of drugs. But let us not assume that it can be used indiscriminately. We know of one case—a woman who was suffering from a serious eye affliction—who thought at first that she was deriving a great deal of benefit from acupuncture, but after several weeks, she developed agonizing headaches immediately after each treatment and the treatments had to be discontinued.

BEE VENOM

Bee venom has been listed among a dozen or so arthritis remedies.

N. Yoirish in his *Curative Properties of Honey and Bee Venom* published in Russia, points out that while there is as yet no theory to explain the therapeutic value of bee venom, it has provided symptomatic relief in rheumatic fever, neuritis, neuralgia, and various other ailments.

Many years ago a fine elderly physician, Dr. Joseph Broadman, wrote a book in which he stressed the benefits of bee venom. We have had no personal experience with the effects of this therapy in the treatment of arthritis, but from what we have learned from one of our associates, it acts as a nonspecific stimulus to the defense mechanism of the body. By stimulating the functions of the pituitary-adrenal axis, it increases the production rate of antibodies, and

* "Acupuncture Anesthesia in People's Republic of China," *Journal of the American Medical Association*, September 2, 1974.

this provides a certain amount of relief. Since it does not cause any of the serious side effects of the pain- and symptom-suppressive drugs, we do not object to its use, but we must not be mistaken in thinking that it offers a cure for the disease. To get the arthritis patient well, the disordered metabolism must be restored to normal, and this can be accomplished only when the health of the entire body is rebuilt.

There are very few practitioners of bee-venom therapy. One who recently has become known to us is Charles Mraz, of Middlebury, Vermont.

WARMTH AND REST

An acutely inflamed and painful joint often obtains relief when it is given the rest it needs and when it is kept warm.

THE YUCCA PLANT IN ARTHRITIS

Recently, a study conducted by Dr. Robert Bingham and Dr. Bernard A. Bellew on about 150 patients who suffered from various types of arthritis, with tablets of the Yucca saponin from the plant that thrives in the Mojave Desert in the Southwest, proved that 56 per cent of those who were kept on these tablets reported considerably less stiffness and crippling, suffered considerably less pain, and showed a reduction in the swelling of the joints.

The extract of this plant is of a fine gelatinous nature and it retains a great deal of water. When taken internally it passes through the human digestive tract without being absorbed and undoubtedly acts as a laxative, but because of its gelatinous nature, is entirely harmless. The investigators were unable to explain how it benefits the arthritis sufferer, but according to Harold J. Taub, editor of *Let's Live,* a monthly health magazine published in the United States, its major effect seems to be on the intestinal flora, "the bacteria that live within the human intestine in a symbiotic relationship."* Since this has a beneficial effect on the diges-

* Let's Live, August, 1975.

tion and keeps in check certain types of harmful bacteria that would otherwise be flourishing in the colon, it helps to improve the health of the whole body and the arthritis sufferer benefits from it.

Every so often we are told of herbal products or remedies that prove helpful in arthritis, and when these products or remedies are harmless to the body as a whole, we see no serious objections to their use, provided those who turn to them realize that their aim must be, not merely to obtain a certain measure of relief, but also to rebuild the overall health of their bodies, since this is the only way arthritis can be overcome or obliterated.

The benefits that were derived by those who were placed on the tablet made from Yucca saponin, only proved anew the correctness of our premise that if the arthritis sufferer is to get well, he must adopt a plan of care that rebuilds the health of the entire body. This proves that what the arthritis patient needs is not a specific remedy for the disease, but a plan of care that normalizes and regulates all bodily functions.

ARTHRITIS AND B-6

A very interesting study on the benefits that arthritic and other rheumatic disease sufferers derive from Vitamin B-6 has been published recently. Dr. John M. Ellis, in his *Vitamin B-6—The Doctor's report,* leaves no doubt in the reader's mind that Vitamin B-6 is highly beneficial for sufferers from these painful and often crippling diseases.

However, as you continue to follow the description of his various explorations, *you cannot help but come to the conclusion that a deficiency or shortage of this vitamin is usually to be found in those whose diet is highly inadequate, or who live on refined and processed foods.* This unhealthful way of living often leads to all kinds of maladies, including arthritis and the other rheumatic diseases.

We do not question the fact that arthritis sufferers require Vitamin B-6. But they also require all the other vitamins—those already well known, as well as those science has not as yet uncovered. In addition, they also require all the other protective elements such as minerals, enzymes, trace elements, etc., and where are they to get all these needs if not in a well-planned, easily digestible nutritional program? We must never forget that food should not be fragmented, and that a deficiency of one basic nutritional element often predisposes us to others.

Dr. Ellis points out that Vitamin B-6 is found most abundantly in the whole grains, fish, milk, eggs, vegetables and yeast. He further mentions wheat germ, pecans, avocados, and then states that among the fruits, bananas are especially rich in Vitamin B-6. He finally stresses the fact that *these foods are best when they are eaten in their uncooked state.* "The longer the green vegetables are boiled, the less food value they have."*

It should be apparent from all this that those who adopt the nutritional program that is stressed in this book will never have to worry about getting an adequate supply of Vitamin B-6, or any of the other nutrients that their body requires, since the foods we advocate provide all the nutrients we need in whole and complete form.

NECK COLLAR RELIEVES NECK PAIN

In this book, we do not stress mere relief of pain, although this must not be overlooked. By keeping the neck warm and limiting its movements, a neck collar made of foam rubber is often helpful, but it should not be worn continuously. Gentle stretching and neck exercises will do much to improve circulation and loosen up stiffened neck joints.

ELASTIC BANDAGES HELP OTHER JOINTS

An elastic bandage carefully wrapped around an acutely painful joint inhibits the movement of the joint and keeps it warm. However, it must be put on with care so that it does

*Vitamin B-6—The Doctor's Report, Dr. John M. Ellis and James Presley. New York: Harper & Row, 1972.

not interfere with circulation. One should be careful not to become too dependent on these bandages, but they are infinitely better than braces or casts because they do not cause complete immobilization and the joint is less likely to become stiffened. While these bandages are used, gentle exercises to improve circulation and prevent the joint from becoming locked, are essential.

LOWER BACK SUPPORT OFTEN HELPFUL

A belt that protects the lower part of the back against excessive strain and friction may be helpful, or a bandage wrapped around the chest and upper part of the back when it is painful and in need of support. These supports provide a certain amount of protection against strain, but should be used only as temporary measures and should be dispensed with when no longer needed.

OTHER HELPFUL TECHNIQUES

Other techniques found to be helpful through the years to sufferers from the arthritic and rheumatic diseases are: Japanese pressure therapy—Shiatsu, Swedish massage, Indian yoga—to name a few. When applied judiciously, they provide relief the natural, healthful way, and many of them contribute to total rebuilding.

CHAPTER 7

A POSITIVE PROGRAM

THE FIRST WEEK

We have been asked to present a 14-day schedule which would illustrate how the sufferer from arthritis should put our program into operation. We questioned its feasibility, since we know that there is more than one road to heaven; there are many, and the one chosen has to conform to what is most suitable or desirable at a particular time or in a particular case, otherwise it might fail.

We do not mean by this that we can ever overlook basic principles. A routine that fails to conform to the tenets outlined in this book, will lead us nowhere. The program, however, must be adjusted to the needs of each individual case. The severity of the disease, the various associated ailments, the effects of medication, the recuperative powers of the individual, as well as the cooperation we can get, often play a part in determining how the regimen is to be applied for effective results.

There are cases that lend themselves to more intensive care, while others may have to follow a slower pattern. It is very much like trying to reach a certain destination. We can walk, or travel by train or car, or we can fly there! It depends on how fast we wish to go, how anxious we are to arrive, and the pace most suitable for the journey. The point we must never overlook, however, is what we are aiming to accomplish, and we must be sure that we are traveling in the right direction.

Although this precludes outlining a routine that could be applied in all instances, it is, nevertheless, possible to present, *merely by way of illustration,* a typical schedule so that the reader can visualize its application in the average case.

HOW DO WE START?
We start with a change in diet.

We pointed out that whenever possible, patients should abstain completely from solid food and subsist only on water, fruit juices, hot vegetable broth or a favorite herb tea, for one, two, or even several days. This is the most effective approach, since it promotes a more intensive elimination of toxins and provides rest to the body's vital organs.

This, however, is not always feasible. Many people have been conditioned to think that they must have three solid meals a day, and that if they omit eating a meal at any time, they are likely to weaken their bodies or undermine their health still further. Because of this, we often find it advisable to start at first with a less drastic program. As an alternative, we start some of these patients on a fruit diet, urging them to take one kind of fruit whenever hungry or about every 2 to 3 hours, or when this seems too drastic we advise a carefully regulated fruit and vegetable diet.

The following is a typical example of such a diet.

7-DAY "START-OFF" DIET
Monday
Breakfast: Raw apple, very ripe banana and cup of alfalfa, camomile or any other bland herb tea, gently sweetened with honey. If hungry between meals, raw fresh fruit, fruit juices, herb teas or vegetable broth are usually permitted.
Lunch: Raw vegetable salad of lettuce, cucumber, grated carrots and celery, baked or boiled unpeeled potatoes and steamed stringbeans, stewed or soaked prunes for dessert.
Never add sugar or sweetening to fruit.

Dinner: Raw vegetable salad of romaine lettuce,* grated raw beetroot, grated parsnips, and green or sweet red peppers, natural brown rice, steamed sprouts, baked or raw sweet apple for dessert. (We reiterate, never add sugar or sweetening to fruit).

Tuesday

Breakfast: Bunch of grapes, small portion of cottage (pot) cheese; alfalfa or any other favorite herb tea, gently sweetened with honey.

Lunch: Raw vegetable salad of chicory, escarole, grated carrots and radishes, natural brown rice or any favorite protein food, ripe pear or other fresh fruit or berries in season for dessert (no added sweetening).

Dinner: Raw vegetable salad of grated carrots, raw grated beetroot, cucumber and celery, baked yams or sweet potatoes, steamed or boiled artichokes, apple sauce made of sweet apples only (no added sweetening).

Wednesday

Breakfast: Large portion of melon, ripe baked bananas, glass of raw, skimmed milk, or any favorite herb tea slightly sweetened with honey.

Lunch: Raw vegetable salad of chicory, celery, watercress and grated carrots, steamed young beans and broccoli, shredded raw sweet apple.

Dinner: Raw vegetable salad of grated cabbage, sweet peppers, celery, cucumber, baked or boiled unpeeled potatoes and steamed eggplant, baked or raw sweet apple or pear.

Thursday

Breakfast: Grated and slightly heated raw apple, unprocessed brown rice, favorite herb tea gently sweetened with honey.

*The English equivalent is cos lettuce.

Lunch: Large fruit salad (fresh fruits only), 4-5 oz. of any soft, bland cheese, fresh fruit juice or a preferred herb tea sparingly honey-sweetened.

Dinner: Raw vegetable salad of diced celery, grated carrots, diced apple and raisins, corn on the cob, steamed onions and celery, stewed or soaked prunes.

Friday

Breakfast: Stewed pears, 1 to 2 slices wholewheat or wholerye toast or 3 to 4 Swedish rye or rice wafers, 1 glass of skimmed, raw milk, or the honey sweetened herb tea.

Lunch: Raw vegetable salad of cut-up spinach leaves, celery, raw grated beetroot, grated Kohlrabi, vegetable stew of young peas, celery and carrot; sweet, raw or baked apple or peaches.

Dinner: Raw vegetable salad of lettuce, green peppers, grated cabbage, grated carrots, baked or boiled unpeeled potatoes, freshly prepared beet soup, fresh fruit compote (no sweetening).

Saturday

Breakfast: Grated, raw sweet apple, slightly heated natural brown rice, honey-sweetened herb tea.

Lunch: Salad of diced celery, diced apples and pears, grapes, a few seedless raisins, served on a bed of lettuce, cottage (pot) cheese, melon in season.

Dinner: Raw vegetable salad of escarole, cucumber, radishes and grated turnips, young, green sweet peas, baked eggplant, shredded raw apple.

Sunday

Breakfast: Bunch of grapes, very ripe banana, glass of raw skimmed milk or honey-sweetened herb tea.

Lunch: Raw vegetable salad of grated carrot, shredded cabbage, diced celery, grated parsnips, water cress, freshly prepared vegetable soup, slice of whole-wheat toast, Swedish rye wafers or rice cakes.

Dinner: Raw vegetable salad of green lettuce, spinach

leaves, grated turnips, baked potato, steamed kale or other greens, apple sauce prepared from sweet apples (no added sweetening).

The above diet is often most suitable for a start. It is not too rigid and gives the person who is not accustomed to dieting a chance to realize that although asked to give up some of the conventional foods, he can still obtain ample nourishment and the meals are pleasurably satisfying. Coffee, tea, sugar, white bread and other white flour products; the refined and processed cereals, cakes, pastries, spicy foods and ingredients rich in hard, hydrogenated fats such as butter, cream, fatty meats, and fatty cheeses are omitted. This schedule is sometimes carried on for another week, or even longer. In many instances, however, after a week of such a careful way of eating, a more radical approach could be suggested.

A fast on water only, or a fruit or vegetable juice or broth diet, is then more readily accepted. Alfalfa, camomile, linden blossom or any of the other tasty herb teas, may also be used and are of great benefit. When a patient finds it difficult to abstain from solid food for a full day, we recommend the use of liquids until evening and then a meal of raw vegetable salad, baked potatoes and one steamed vegetable. When fresh fruits are used, the patient should eat only one kind of fruit at a time, and only fruits in season.

VALUE OF LIQUID DIETS

At this point it is well to reiterate that when the patient is in the throes of an acute attack, the benefits that can be derived from a liquid diet, i.e., fruit juice, vegetable juices, vegetable broth, and herb teas, or even a complete fast for a short period, taking nothing but water when desired, must not be overlooked. Such a program, for a limited time, need not frighten us. These dietary restrictions have now become quite fashionable in some medical circles, since they have proved of inestimable value to those in search of health.

OTHER PARTS OF THE PROGRAM

We are certain that by this time, those who need help realize that while a change in nutrition is essential in these cases, this represents only part of the program. We mentioned that some patients suffer from constipation, and if this is the case, warm, cleansing enemas are recommended to relieve the condition. Hot, epsom salt baths and properly planned exercises are also offered as part of the regular routine.

When enemas are needed, it is often advisable to start with one a day for the first two to three days, and one every second day for about a week. Later, they should be reduced to one about every third or fourth day and should be discontinued when the bowels begin to move regularly. In the meantime, attempts to establish normal bowel functioning must be made. As we have mentioned on many occasions, those who eat three meals a day will soon find that they can move their bowels at least twice and often three times daily.

The hot, epsom salt bath is to be taken daily at first. If enemas are needed and are taken in the evening, they should always be taken before the bath—not after. Following the bath, the patient should immediately retire and make sure to be well covered. If this induces perspiration, it is to be welcomed since this indicates that the body is eliminating toxins by way of the skin.

Exercises are suggested twice daily, mornings upon rising, and evenings before taking the bath. We usually start with deep breathing. This is followed by the milder leg raising routine, and any of the other exercises that do not overtire the patient and can be performed according to the limitations of each case. The movements described in the chapter on exercises may be followed.

Exercises should be increased gradually, but should never be carried to the point of fatigue.

OTHER POINTS TO REMEMBER

We always insist on an abundance of rest and sleep.

Whenever possible, we urge a rest period or nap after the noon meal. In some cases, a rest period or a nap after each meal is very helpful. All tensions and excitements must be eliminated or reduced to a minimum. It should not be difficult to understand that emotional upsets impair the health of the patient still further, and interfere with recovery.

Since one of the problems in this disease is poor circulation, the feet must be kept warm at all times. We urge the wearing of appropriate foot gear and, whenever necessary, recommend that a hot water bottle or an electric heating pad be applied to the feet.

This, in essence, is a sample of our program at the start. It is essential to remember that patience is required. No doctor or drug ever cures arthritis—the healing powers of the body do the curing. The patient must understand what has to be done to give the body a chance to get well—*and then go ahead and do it!* He or she must also realize that the time it takes to get well does not depend upon a specific remedy but upon the amount of damage, the body's ability to bring about the necessary correction, and one's own willingness to cooperate. Sound guidance by one skilled in this type of care is of great help, since it provides the necessary encouragement and enables the patient to carry out the program in accordance with his particular needs. However, where experienced guidance is not readily available, the patient must still rely on this care, if lasting benefits are to be attained.

THE SECOND WEEK

In some cases the diet outlined above is continued for more than one week, sometimes for two weeks or even longer; it takes some patients longer than others to adjust themselves to this new way of eating. In the great majority of cases, however, a single week is sufficient to convince them that even though certain undesirable foods and beverages have been eliminated, the diet is nevertheless adequate and provides ample nourishment, as well as a great sense of well-being.

Once we have reached this point we are prepared for the next step, and the fast days or the liquid diet can then be introduced. Here is an example of the routine for the following week, or, when necessary, two or three weeks later.

Monday

A liquid diet. The patient is advised to take only water whenever desired, or a glass of freshly-squeezed orange juice, grapefruit or apple juice, hot vegetable broth, or any of the herb teas.

Tuesday

Breakfast: one kind of raw fruit only—apple, pear, melon, grapes, or any of the other fresh fruit in season, honey-sweetened herb tea.

Lunch: Raw vegetable salad of lettuce, celery, cucumber and grated carrots, steamed squash and carrots, grapefruit or any other fresh, baked or stewed fruits (no sugar or other sweetening).

Dinner: Raw vegetable salad of escarole, chicory or other greens, grated parsnips, grated beetroot, radishes, baked potato and steamed okra or squash, baked apple (unsweetened).

Wednesday

Breakfast: As on Tuesday.

Lunch: Fresh fruit salad, any of the fresh fruits in season, 4-5 oz. of cottage cheese, or any soft, bland goat cheese or other favorite protein food. (Many of the better health food stores usually supply a bland and easily digestible goat cheese).

Dinner: Raw vegetable salad of romaine (cos) lettuce or other greens, grated carrots, grated turnips, watercress, baked or boiled unpeeled potato, steamed or baked artichoke, steamed or soaked, unsulphured apricots.

Thursday

Repeat the liquid diet as on Monday.

Friday
Breakfast: Any fresh fruit, honey-sweetened herb tea, or a glass of skimmed milk. (When skimmed milk is suggested, clabbered milk, yogurt, or buttermilk may be substituted.)*

Lunch: Salad of lettuce or other green vegetable, tomatoes, cucumber and celery, modest portion of pot or goat cheese, ½ grapefruit or any other raw fruit.

Dinner: Raw vegetable salad of escarole, lettuce or other greens, grated parsnips, grated carrots, chopped or diced parsley, baked sweet potato or yam, steamed green peas, stewed, unsulphured peaches.

Saturday
Breakfast: Shredded, slightly heated apple, portion of organically grown brown rice, honey-sweetened herb tea.

Lunch: Salad of grated carrots, diced celery, diced apple, a few raisins, 4 to 5 oz. of any of the soft, bland cheeses or any other favorite protein food, ½ grapefruit or any other raw fruit.

Dinner: Raw vegetable salad of romaine (cos) lettuce, diced escarole, grated turnips, grated carrot, baked or boiled unpeeled potato, steamed string beans, compote made of fresh fruits (pears, apples, peaches, prunes; add a few raisins for sweetening). No sugar or other sweetening should be used.

Sunday
Breakfast: Dish of stewed or soaked peaches, a ready-prepared wholegrain cereal. (These cereals are sold at all health food stores). A cup of raw, skimmed milk or honey-sweetened herb tea.

Lunch: Diced celery, grated carrots, sliced tomatoes, 4 to 5 oz. of any bland cheeses as mentioned above, or any other favorite protein food, cup of hot vegetable soup.

*In some cases of arthritis—especially rheumatoid arthritis—allergy is suspected, and if this is the case, dairy products may have to be omitted entirely. Small portions of other easily digested protein foods may be substituted.

Dinner: Raw vegetable salad of chicory, parsley, other greens, grated turnip, grated kohlrabi, steamed wild or brown rice with diced celery and carrots, any freshly stewed fruit for dessert.

In some cases, the liquid diet may have to be restricted to only one day, while in other cases it may be extended over a longer period of time, even several days in succession. Where patients find it too difficult to abstain from solid food for a whole day, we suggest a liquid diet until evening, and then a meal similar to those outlined above.

The meals may be interchanged and one vegetable substituted for another. For those who are hungry between meals, any fresh fruit, fruit or vegetable juices, or cup of a favorite herb tea is permitted. Moderate amounts of raw, freshly extracted vegetable juices between meals are often suggested for valuable added nourishment.

The above program illustrates the idea that is usually followed in these cases. Of course, it can be adjusted to meet individual problems. Associated disturbances have to be considered in planning the diet, while the likes and dislikes of the patient must not be overlooked.

To avoid misunderstanding, we wish to emphasize that this program represents but the start of a regimen that must be followed consistently over an extended period of time, if permanent results are to be attained.

CHAPTER 8

AVOID HEAVY PROTEINS AND FATS

You will note that among the protein foods, lean fish or chicken, soft bland cheeses, small amounts of seeds and nuts are listed as permissible, but we rarely, if ever, mention meat, especially beef. In any form, beef contains harmful amounts of uric acid, and is therefore particularly harmful in arthritic and rheumatic diseases. The hard saturated fats in meat contribute to the accumulation of excessive amounts of cholesterol and other fat substances in the blood. As is known, these factors compound the problems of arthritic or rheumatic diseases and are detrimental to health generally. A report recently issued by a cancer research team headed by Dr. William Haensel pointed out that in 1974, 100,000 Americans would develop bowel cancer, and that the long chain of saturated fatty acids in beef play a considerable role in the onset of this type of cancer.*

Another cancer specialist, Dr. Ernest Wynder, President of the American Health Foundation, New York City, pointed to the need of limiting the intake of fatty meats and eggs (also the dairy fats), since "this would not only help prevent the half a million premature deaths from heart disease, but also reduce deaths from colon rectal cancer."**

*Newsweek, Feb. 18, 1974, "Beef and Bowel Cancer."
**New York Times, March 25, 1974, "Low Fat, Low Cholesterol Diet Called Positive."

It should be obvious that any kind of food that contributes to death from cardiovascular diseases and cancer, is also detrimental to those who suffer from the acutely painful and crippling arthritic and rheumatic diseases.

DO VEGETABLES PROVIDE THE PROTEIN WE NEED?

This question is often asked, and in reply, we point out that those who follow a carefully regulated nutritional program need not worry whether they get the correct amount and right kind of protein; this holds true even for those who abstain from meat entirely. The finest protein comes from plant life—from the fruit and vegetable kingdom—although in less concentrated form. An excess of protein is known to be harmful.

Recently Dr. Glenn D. Toppenberg, of the New England Memorial Hospital, Stoneham, Massachusetts, referred to the findings of Drs. I. H. Pope and J. Stamler and pointed out that in a report on diet and coronary disease, these authorities made it clear that in populations habitually subsisting on diets high in animal foodstuffs, including dairy products, the lesion (atherosclerosis) and the disease (heart disease) were invariably common. In contrast, *populations with predominantly vegetarian diets had low occurrence rates* (emphasis ours).

Dr. Toppenberg quoted the studies of John W. Berg and others of the National Cancer Institute, as well as the findings of Lemon and Walden who pointed out that the health of the Seventh Day Adventists, who are vegetarians, is of a much higher level than the health of those who follow a conventional diet.

Others who corroborate Dr. Toppenberg's view are Dr. Robert Rigsby and Dr. Robert Statz, of the same hospital.*

Another doctor who wondered whether the vegetarian way of living would not be more desirable, was Louis V.

*"Vegetarian Diet," *Journal of the American Medical association,* April 22, 1974.

Avioli, M.D., professor of medicine at Washington School of Medicine. In a talk at a conference attended by more than 800 men and women in medicine, nursing and teaching, sponsored by the Institute of Human Nutrition, College of Physicians and Surgeons, Columbia University, Dr. Avioli stated that sufferers from osteoporosis require protein, but not animal protein, and added, "maybe we should all be vegetarians."*

We stress this because it is important to know that meat is not essential to health, and that those who adopt a vegetarian diet need not feel that they are deprived of essential nutrients, provided they adhere to the type of diet we stress in this book. We do not insist that sufferers from arthritis become vegetarians, although this is to be preferred. But those who wish to include meat in their diet are advised to limit their intake to small amounts of lean fish, fowl or the soft cheeses.

THE BENEFITS OF VEGETARIANISM

Not much later, *Today's Health,* a journal published for the public by the American Medical Association, described the benefits derived from a carefully planned vegetarian diet. It reminded us that the word vegetarianism comes from the Latin "vegetus," which means "whole, sound, fresh, lively." Studies conducted by leading investigators proved that a sensible vegetarian diet builds a higher standard of health and helps to protect us against many of the chronic and degenerative diseases.

Outlined below, are a few of the significant points made in the article.

LOWER CHOLESTEROL LEVELS

In a study conducted by Dr. Frederick Stare, Department of Nutrition, Harvard School of Public Health, and Dr. Mervyn Hardings, Dean of the Loma Linda School of

New York Times, November 22, 1975.

Health, it is proved that vegetarians have consistently lower cholesterol levels than have meat eaters. Because an overload of cholesterol contributes to the development of hypertension, heart disease, diabetes, kidney, liver and gall-bladder diseases, even cancer, this finding is highly significant.

THE DANGER OF MEAT ADDITIVES AND PRESERVATIVES

Dr. Charles Edwards, formerly Commissioner of the Food and Drug Administration, now Secretary of Health in the Department of Health, Education and Welfare, has pointed out that chemicals such as sodium nitrite used as preservatives in meat, are "potentially dangerous, even carcinogenic."

DES (diethylstilbesterol), a hormone fed or implanted in cattle to spur their growth, also has a harmful effect on our bodies; it too has been labeled carcinogenic (cancer producing).

ANIMAL PROTEIN CAUSES PUTREFACTIVE CHANGES IN INTESTINAL TRACT

U. D. Register, Chairman of the Nutrition Department of the Loma Linda School of Health, has been quoted as saying that "animal protein tends to create anaerobic bacteria in the intestinal tract and these anaerobic bacteria tend to convert bile acids into carcinogenic compounds." In other words, by changing bile acids into cancer producing compounds these bacteria contribute to the onset of cancer.*

As we keep pointing out, the arthritis sufferer has to adopt a plan of care that helps to rebuild the health of the entire body, and a change to a carefully regulated vegetarian diet is recommended.

*"Here's What you Should Know About Vegetarianism," by Daniel Grotta-Kurska.

CHAPTER 9

SPROUTING UNLOCKS VITAL NUTRIENTS

Don't miss sprouts. Sprouting unlocks vital nutrients and enriches meals in an infinite number of ways. Sprouted seeds are alive with minerals, vitamins and enzymes.

The following are some of the seeds that can be sprouted successfully:

Seeds: Alfalfa, sunflower, sesame, red clover.

Grains: Wheat, rye, oats, corn, barley.

Dried Beans and Peas: Mungbeans, soybeans, green peas, lentils, garbanzo beans (or chickpeas), azuki beans, marrow beans, kidney beans, pinto beans, fava beans.

All seeds are suitable for sprouting, but make sure that they are of the highest quality. *They should not be too old; if possible they should be organically grown, and they should not have been chemically treated.*

EXTOLLING SPROUTS

Beatrice Trum Hunter, a highly regarded nutritionist who has devoted years of study to the subject of nutrition, extols the virtues of sprouts by telling us that as well as providing valuable nutrition, they are also easy to grow in one's own home. They require no special tools or gadgets, they involve no backbreaking labor, weeding, or anxiety about insect pests, yet they can provide a crop of crisp fresh vegetables daily.

Of course you must not take this to mean that sprouts are to take the place of the large raw vegetable salad we urge our patients to have at least once a day. Sprouts should be used as an addition to the variety of vegetables that are grown in the soil and that contain the vital nutrients that we need for health.

Among the seeds that Mrs. Hunter favors are alfalfa, red clover and fenugreek. She mentions that they are ready to be eaten when they are one to two inches long. She also mentions mungbeans, ready to be eaten when they are one and one-half inches long; lentils, peas and radishes, ready to be eaten when they are one inch long, and wheat berry sprouts, ready to be eaten when one-fourth to one-half inch long.

She tells that there are two schools of thought—whether growing sprouts should be placed in a dark cupboard, or be exposed to light. Then she informs us that those which are grown in the cupboard develop more Vitamin C, while those exposed to light develop more chlorophyll and are better tasting. She favors those exposed to light, but not to direct sunlight. She says, "Sprouts are not an especially high or dependable source of Vitamin C," and favors the chlorophyll and the flavor factor. She does point out, how-ever, that soybean sprouts do better in the dark.

She warns that potato sprouts should be avoided because they are poisonous.

SPROUTING ALFALFA SEEDS, LENTILS, RYE AND WHEAT BERRIES

Another esteemed nutritionist, Jane Kinderlehrer, in the March, 1974 issue of *Prevention,* a monthly publication de-voted to health and nutrition, explains how easy it is to do your own sprouting.

Place one tablespoonful of alfalfa seeds, or three table-spoons of lentils, rye or wheat berries in a quart jar. Add enough water to make the jar half full. Cover and let stand overnight. The next morning cover the jar with a double layer of cheese cloth, a nylon net, or a screened cover obtainable in health food stores and drain off the water. But don't discard it since it contains valuable nutrients and can be used for soups or in preparing grains and vegetables.

After pouring off the first water, rinse the seeds, grains or legumes. But again, don't discard this water either. (If you have plants in your home, feed this water to the plants and they'll love you for it.)

Invert the jar or tilt it sufficiently so that any moisture still in it can drain off. Then place the jar in a dark place, under the sink or any place where it is dark and warm. To get seeds to sprout well, they need moisture, warmth and darkness. Repeat the rinsing about two or three times a day.

Alfalfa seeds take about five days until they are ready to be eaten. Jane Kinderlehrer mentions that after about the third day in the jar, the seeds have a tendency to clump together. To unclump them, dump them into a large bowl filled with water and carefully separate them. Replace them gently in the jar, and as soon as two tiny leaves appear take the jar from the dark place and expose it to the light. This makes the leaves turn green, and you know that they are overflowing with chlorophyll and are ready to be eaten. Be sure to eat the whole sprout, the old seed, the shell, the tiny root, the stem, the leaves—everything.

Here, as you see, Jane starts her sprouting in the dark and then follows it up by exposing it to the light.

The grains and lentils are ready to be eaten by about the end of the second day. Don't let the wheat sprouts grow any longer than the grain itself. Jane reminds us that sprouts continue to grow, even after they are placed in the refrigerator and right up to the moment they are on your salad plate.

SPROUTING GARBANZO BEANS

Lentils, pinto beans, kidney beans, azuki beans, fava beans, black-eyed peas, and garbanzo beans (or chick peas), all can be sprouted and then used as valuable additions to our meals. Garbanzo beans, as Jane points out, are rich in potassium and low in sodium, and this ration makes them especially valuable for the heart muscle. They also provide a supply of iron, calcium, phosphorus, vitamin A, niacin, thiamin and riboflavin. And when sprouted, these nutrients multiply innumerable times. Another valuable vitamin they supply is B_{12}.

In sprouting legumes, care is necessary. Legumes need a great deal of space and cannot be crowded. Here is how she suggests that garbanzo beans be sprouted.

Soak a half cup of garbanzo beans overnight. Use plenty of water since these beans grow more than double in volume. Next morning, pour off the liquid and save it for soup stock. Then rinse the garbanzo beans and spread them out on a soup plate in a single layer and cover plate with several layers of dampened paper toweling. Slip the plate into a plastic bag to retain moisture. Keep in a fairly warm place and make sure that the paper toweling is always moist. Sprinkle with water a couple of times a day if necessary and wash the beans once or twice daily to wash off molds.

Sprouting them in a collander instead of a soup plate makes it even easier. All you have to do is to spray the beans right over the paper toweling two or three times a day and then the collander can be left in the sink to drain. Either one of these methods will provide a fine crop of garbanzo sprouts in 2 or 3 days.

Many books on sprouting are obtainable in the major health food stores, and most health food stores also carry special equipment to make sprouting a fine and most joyous experience. Get started!

CHAPTER 10

THE NEED FOR PHYSIOLOGIC REST

We have already mentioned that chronic fatigue is an outstanding characteristic in many arthritis cases, and therefore, patients require a great deal of rest and sleep. However, mere physical repose is not sufficient to overcome the existing fatigue. Various toxic influences often contribute to the state of weariness, and all these harmful factors must be eliminated if the patient is to get well. When the vital functions are overtaxed by wrong or excessive food; when tensions and stresses deplete body energy, and when the stimulating but health-debilitating habits that are so much a part of the average person's way of living are persisted in, a toxic condition inevitably develops, and this ultimately creates a state of chronic fatigue.

Smoking, drinking, late hours, are some of the more common abuses. If the toxic condition is to be really overcome, all the causes that contributed to its development must be eliminated or corrected. This explains why a change in our living habits is essential. It further explains why we stress the need for periodic fasts, or the more restricted diets, as well as an overall carefully planned dietary regimen. In making these changes, the body is provided with a plenitude of what is sometimes called a much-needed "physiologic rest," and this goes far towards overcoming the toxic condition, as well as the various existing disturbances.

The term "physiologic rest" may sound strange to some of our readers, and so we hasten to explain that the body is provided with sufficient rest, not merely when we obtain adequate physical rest and sleep, but also when we make certain not to overtax the internal organs of the body.

By discontinuing all health-debilitating practices, we reduce the strain upon the body, giving it a chance to rest and regain some of its strength and vitality.

Changes in our living habits also diminish the burden placed upon the heart, liver, circulation, and the glands of internal secretions such as the thyroid gland, the adrenal glands and the pituitary gland. This in turn encourages more efficient functioning of the organs.

Such modifications will also reduce body exertion and provide much needed rest for strengthening and rebuilding. Physical or body relaxation, as well as the rest that is obtained when the work of the internal organs is reduced, are essential if arthritis or any of the other rheumatic diseases are to be overcome.

PHYSICAL EXERCISE IMPORTANT

The need for physical as well as physiologic rest does not mean, however, that physical exercises are to be written off as unimportant. A tired and weary body suffers greatly from stagnation and sluggishness, and when this continues over a prolonged period of time it leads only to further atrophy and greater crippling. In our earlier writings on this disease, we quoted Dr. Ralph K. Ghormley, who pointed out that an examination of the tissues by surgical procedure in cases where physical activity has not been arrested, disclosed that the tissues are healthy and smooth. "These surfaces (the smooth surfaces of contact between the fascia and underlying muscle), fairly glisten and are not adherent," Dr. Ghormley writes. He continues: "On the other hand, when one opens a thigh that has been at rest either in

a cast or in a splint, or as a result of rest in bed, one finds
that the fascial surface, as well as the surface of the underlying muscle, is dull and does not glide; often times, many
small adhesions have formed between the muscle and
fascia."*

Many surgeons recognize the value of physical activities.
I.L. Lichtenstein, who specializes in hernia surgery with local anaesthesia, insists that immediately upon the comple-
tion of his operation, the patient starts walking. Within a
day or two he is encouraged to return to all his normal activities, with the only proviso that he not overdo, and rest
when tired. Dr. Lichtenstein quotes Dumphy and Jackson,
who (in the *American Journal of Surgery, 104, 273, 1962*)
stress "the importance of use and strain on the factors
which lead to the attainment of optimal tensile strength" in
tissue repair.

They go on to say: "The changes of physical state and
tissue orientation are probably a physico-chemical phe-
nomenon which cannot be influenced greatly except by
use."

Dr. Lichtenstein adds that from his observation it would
appear that "immediate ambulation and return to ordinary
physical activity not only does not interfere with wound
healing, but may actually promote the tensile strength of
the surgical wound."**

While the above-quoted authorities were not discussing
the joint or rheumatic diseases that we are covering in this
book, the point they are making regarding the need for activity and motion to counteract stagnation and maintain a
condition favorable for the promotion of healing and repair,
must never be overlooked.

It is essential to remember that while the need for rest
has to be stressed as part of the overall rebuilding program,
the right kind of exercises must be encouraged. Muscular

*"The Abuse of Rest in Bed in Orthopedic Surgery," *J.A.M.A.*, Aug 19,
1941.
**"Local Anesthesia for Hernia," *California Medicine,* February 1964.

inactivity or any organic inactivity over an extended period of time, leads only to further deterioration and hampers recovery. Where the patient is handicapped because of disease or breakdown, an alert physician will adjust exercises to the needs of the particular case, to check further deterioration and promote repair. Dr. Gordon M. Martin, in an editorial in the *Journal of the American Medical Association,* June 6, 1966, commenting on a study that was published in the same issue of the *Journal* on the subject of inactivity, sagely remarks that "awareness of the hazards of inactivity can well become a stimulus to every physician to limit inactivity and immobilization to the essential minimum and at the same time set goals for desirable amounts of exercise and activity."

A similar report came through only recently. Dr. R. Bruce Heppenstall, appearing at a meeting of the Society of the University of Surgeons in St. Louis, Missouri, stressed the fact that "to promote wound healing in patients who have been subjected to severe trauma . . . cardiac output must be boosted above normal levels to significantly increase the wound tissue oxygen." He then pointed out that oxygen concentration affects the healing process and that "a diminished supply of oxygen decreases the rate of repair and increases susceptibility to infection."

Since weakened and broken-down joints need an increased supply of oxygen if they are to regain their health, the view expressed by Dr. Heppenstall as well as the other scientists whom we have quoted above must not be overlooked.

The latest on this subject, dealing with bone health specifically, comes from Dr. Louis V. Avioli, to whom we referred earlier. Dr. Avioli points out that osteoporosis—the loss of bone that contributes to fractures suffered by older people (and also present in many of the advanced stages of arthritis), is found four times as frequently in women past 35 as in men. The reason for this, as he states it, is conjectural, but then he lists that "dietary indiscretion, decrease in muscle mass, hormonal imbalance, renal dysfunction, have been implicated as causative factors; that certain drugs "leech out mineral from the bone," and that alcohol ingestion ultimately leads to the loss of bone.

Dr. Avioli continues by saying that muscle mass seems very important to the integrity of bone," and then points out that "day to day muscle pulling (exercise) . . . stimulates the formulation of bone."*

Without adequate exercise, deterioration is bound to set in. Stagnation simply cannot be permitted in these cases, and therefore a program of physical exercises conforming to the needs and abilities of the patient, must be encouraged.

The following is a series of exercises that will be of great help. They should be introduced gradually, and increased as the patient's health and strength improve.

DEEP-BREATHING EXERCISES

1. Lie flat on your back on hard surface or floor. Keep mouth closed and inhale slowly and deeply through both nostrils. Hold breath as long as possible and then exhale slowly. This exercise should be repeated five times and then be gradually increased to ten times. Those who are extremely debilitated may not be able to do it more than two or three times at first, but should slowly increase the number until they reach the full count of ten.

2. The same breaths should be taken and expelled through each nostril separately. Block one nostril with your finger and breathe in through the other.

WHY DEEP-BREATHING EXERCISES?

Why are deep-breathing exercises helpful? Because they release tension, help to build body tone, improve general circulation, promote the elimination of toxins, aid in the digestion and assimilation of food. They expand the chest muscles, exercise the muscles of the diaphragm, and pro-

*Nutritional Problems of Women Discussed by Medical Experts, *New York Times,* 11/22/75.

vide an increased supply of oxygen which strengthens and rebuilds the health of the body.

LEG-RAISING EXERCISES

Lie flat on hard surface or floor, as above. Relax completely. Without bending the knee, raise one leg slowly, as far as it will reach; then lower slowly until the floor is touched. Rest for a few seconds and repeat three times, gradually increasing to five and then to ten times.

Repeat the same sequence with the other leg, then with both legs. Always remember that these movements have to be done slowly and that the knees have to be kept straight. We wish to emphasize that those who are extremely weak or debilitated may not be able to do them more than once or twice at first, but they should be increased as the patient grows stronger.

ADVANCED LEG-RAISING EXERCISES

Lie flat on floor or hard surface, as above. Relax completely. Raise one leg slowly, then swing it over first to one side, then to the other, as far as it will reach. Now return leg to center and lower it slowly until you touch the floor. Do this exercise three times; then repeat it with the other leg. Repeat the same exercise with both legs, raising both legs and swinging both of them over, first to one side, then to the other, ultimately bringing them back to the center and lowering them slowly. For some, raising the two legs together may at first be too strenuous. Where this is the case, only the exercises with each leg separately should be done initially, while those involving both legs should be tried later, when more flexibility and greater control has been developed.

KNEE EXERCISES

Lie flat on hard surface, as above. Flex both knees. Now swing each knee slowly outward, then inward, bringing them slowly together again. Repeat at first five to ten times and gradually increase to twenty-five or thirty times.

What do we accomplish with leg and knee exercises? They improve the circulation of the extremities and strengthen the muscles of the lower part of the back. They loosen up rigidity and tension in the joints of the lower regions of the body, tone up the musculature of the abdominal wall as well as the abdominal organs, and do much to rebuild the general circulation.

FEET STRENGTHENING EXERCISES

1. While lying on your back, move feet slowly up and down, as far as possible. Repeat ten times.

2. Same position. Swing feet in and out from the ankles. Make sure to start the movement from the ankles, keeping the upper part of the legs passive. Repeat ten times. These exercises improve the circulation to the feet, loosen up tension, and tone up the muscles of the extremities.

TOE EXERCISE

1. Stand up on your feet and slowly grasp a pencil or marble with your toes. Now release and repeat ten times.

2. While standing, rise up and down on your toes ten times.

What do the feet and toe exercises accomplish? The extremities are often afflicted by arthritis or other forms of rheumatism and sometimes are badly crippled. These movements do much to improve circulation, tone up the distorted muscles and provide greater freedom of motion.

NECK EXERCISES

1. Sit up straight. Bend neck slowly to one side, trying to reach shoulder as far as possible, then bend to the other side. Repeat five times.

2. Rotate neck slowly as far as you can to one side, then to the other side. Repeat five times.

3. Stretch neck forward as far as you can. Repeat five times.

Arthritis and other rheumatic disorders often settle in the neck joints and cause a great deal of pain. These pains often radiate to the head, facial muscles and shoulders. The above exercises stretch and loosen up tightened muscles in the neck, improve circulation, and do much to bring relief to the painful areas of the head, face and shoulders.

EXERCISES SHOULD BE DONE SLOWLY

Always start with the easier movements and then advance to the more strenuous ones. Every phase should be extended as far as the body permits, and all exercises should be done slowly and rhythmically. Some prefer to perform them to music, and to this there is no objection. In time, the muscles become more supple, movements freer.

Improvement in muscle tone, better circulation and greater freedom of mobility, are brought about by these exercises. For maximum results, they should be performed regularly—at least once, or better still, twice daily.

Other exercises may be added in accordance with the need of the case. Whenever possible, they should be carried out under proper supervision. And never, never do them to the point where you become fatigued. If necessary, rest between exercises.

Walking is a fine form of exercise and should, whenever possible, be planned as part of the regular routine.

EARLY CARE A BLESSING

The case histories presented in this book show that even those who suffer from the most difficult forms of arthritis or its allied diseases can often regain their health when they follow a program based upon the use of good, wholesome food and other sound health measures. What a blessing if sufferers would realize the futility of resorting to drugs and instead adopt the program of care suggested early enough to prevent further damage! The suffering and misery that could be avoided is inestimable!

In the early stages of the disease, the pains or discomforts are as a rule not severe enough to cause much worry. Cracking or creaking of the joints, fleeting pains, mere numbness or other indications of distress, are usually some of the early warning signs. At this stage, acute pains may last for a short time and often disappear of their own accord. When they reappear, they sometimes show up in another joint or in a completely different part of the body. If those who are subject to these transient or recurring pains would understand what these symptoms indicate and take the necessary steps to bring about correction, they could save themselves untold pain and misery.

Unfortunately, this is rarely done. The early symptoms are often completely disregarded, or when they become too annoying they are usually treated by some conventional remedy such as aspirin or other pain-relieving drug. It is only when the disease becomes severe and the pains excruciating, that the search for help begins. Then more aspirin, sometimes codeine, later gold injections, and ultimately cortisone or some other related hormones are introduced in an effort to obtain relief. Some patients travel to spas and various health resorts, while others try a variety of physiotherapy treatments.

A point seldom recognized cannot be repeated too often; unless the underlying causes of the disease are eliminated and a program of care along sound hygienic principles is planned, no permanent correction can be expected; the disease is only bound to progress further. It is also essential to emphasize that since the remedies employed in the treatment of these ills are toxic, they create more damage, although in the interim they may reduce pain. These diseases must not be written off as incurable; lasting results can be obtained provided the principles laid down in this book are adhered to. Needless to say, all drugs *must be eliminated.*

CHAPTER 11

WHAT TO EXPECT DURING THE TRANSITION PERIOD

Countless former sufferers from arthritis, or one of its allied diseases, who have succeeded in regaining their health are living examples of the fact that such ailments are not incurable, and that the right kind of care can lead to recovery. Time and patience are required if results are to be attained, and one must not become frightened or lose courage when, during the curative phase, various acute reactions begin to show up. These merely indicate that the body's curative processes are actively engaged in an effort to counteract or overcome the existing disorder. Instead of being feared, they must be understood and everything possible done to help the body accomplish its purpose.

Recurring pains, swelling of the joints, shifting of pains from one part of the body to another; other acute reactions such as fever, skin eruptions, dizziness, nausea, headaches, etc., often manifest themselves during the acute curative phase.

Reactions vary in degrees of severity depending upon the extent of the disease, existing associated disorders, and the recuperative powers of the individual patient. The amount of suppression and the demoralizing effect of the drugs used in the past, undoubtedly play a role in determining the severity and nature of the reactions.

THE DIFFERENCE BETWEEN CHRONIC AND ACUTE DISEASES

At this point it is appropriate that we spend a few minutes explaining the difference between a chronic and an acute disease. In the latter case, the various protective functions of the body are actively engaged in an effort to overcome a toxic or otherwise abnormal condition, and the acute symptoms that are experienced (fever, rapid pulse, inflammation, pain, etc.), only indicate that the body is endeavoring to cope with a condition that is uncongenial or harmful to life.

Sufferers from chronic disease must never forget that acute reactions are healing crises and should not be suppressed.

Patients may sometimes be tempted to resume their former pain-relieving drugs, but should remember that they provide only temporary relief and may lead to more disease and greater suffering. The sooner we realize that this only interferes with the efforts of the body to correct an abnormal condition, the sooner do we find the path to real health. It must be kept in mind that chronic diseases usually develop slowly, often imperceptibly. Usually they progress—not in a straight line—but in zig-zag fashion. As in a tug-of-war, the opposing forces of health and disease keep pulling in opposite directions.

REACTIONS, STEPS ON THE ROAD TO RECOVERY

Many ups and downs are to be expected. Periods of relief may alternate with periods of renewed pain; relief in one joint may be followed by acute flare-ups of pain in other joints, while a variety of other symptoms often show up at one time or another as part of the curative process. These are steps on the road to recovery.

When an acute reaction occurs, it may sometimes come on suddenly and be severe enough to be frightening, as happened while we were taking care of Mildred S.

When we were treating seventy-year-old Agnes C. for rheumatoid arthritis, her ankles, too, filled up with fluid, but in her case the reaction was of a much milder nature; consequently, there was no need for alarm. We'll let Agnes tell the story:

"Just as I was shedding the acute phase, and a change was noted for the better, I suddenly began to experience a regression. Water had accumulated in both ankles to mid-calf, and again my walking was inhibited. Dr. Warmbrand advised that it was a phase of change in circulation. He prescribed cold compresses applied on each ankle, to be covered by oil silk or other plastic material; then to be wrapped in flannel or blanket material to enable it to get warm. These compresses became hot by morning and gradually the swelling markedly reduced. My husband applied these compresses daily for 240 days. I might add there was considerable fluid in both legs, but they finally returned to normal with improved circulation.

"I am compelled to say that every joint and muscle in my body was affected by this affliction in varying degree, including my hands and toes. My right arm, hand and wrist had a supporting sling for over a month; my fingers were practically frozen and I couldn't separate them. All this has changed. I am now able to play classical music on the piano, which aids therapeutically and is no end of pleasure. In all kinds of weather I walk at least a mile a day, and have very little difficulty in mounting a bus.

"I can't emphasize enough the uncertainty and unpredictability of the sudden and sweeping changes that occurred in my body. I was never free from pain, and it constantly shifted from one member to another. In faithfully following Dr. Warmbrand's instructions, with the passage of time it would appear that now I am on the threshold of full recovery.

"This has been a long and painful experience, with the expectation at the onset of no release from my constant misery and suffering.

"The rule of change is simple. Guidance, dedication, patience, with divine assistance is the only answer. I was exceedingly fortunate to meet a healer who could help me. His

constant advice, encouragement, kindness, and friendly ad-
monitions to be patient, changed the course of things.''

As we can see, by persisting with her care, the swelling in
Agnes C.'s ankles ultimately cleared up, and by now she is
well in every way.

HEADACHE OFTEN A TEMPORARY REACTION

Do not become frightened when starting on your health
regimen, or even sometimes later, if you develop a headache. This often happens when the body, adapting itself to
this new regimen, releases a great many toxins that have to
be eliminated. The best and quickest way to clear up a
headache is to take a warm cleansing enema; follow this
with a comfortably hot epsom salt bath, and then apply a
cold compress to the forehead, a hot water bottle to the
back of the head, and try to sleep. Also make sure that your
feet are kept warm. A few hours later, or at most by the
next day, the headache should be gone.

FEVER PART OF THE CURATIVE PROCESS

In arthritis, fever often shows up as part of the body's
curative process. It's one of the body's own defense reactions. In many cases the fever may limit itself to a particular joint, while in others it may show up as a generalized fever involving the entire body. These fevers must not be
feared; they should actually be welcomed since they indicate that the body's own curative powers are endeavoring
to make the necessary adjustments. The body is going
through a much needed housecleaning; it is bringing about
certain changes that help to resolve and ultimately eliminate excess deposits of calcium, as well as the various toxic
waste products that contributed to the onset of the diseased
condition. At the same time, it is also preparing the ground-
work for a thorough rebuilding.

WEAKNESS TEMPORARY

There are those who when changing from conventional
habits of living to our healthful way of living begin to feel a

sense of weakness or debility. This often shows up, not because of inadequate nutrition, but because the overirritating and overstimulating foods and beverages such as coffee, sugar, bread; the refined and processed grain foods; also beef, have been discontinued. Then we begin to find out how debilitated and weakened the body really is. This only proves that what is needed is care that rebuilds, regenerates, and renews our strength. The right kind of food, an abundance of sleep and rest, emotional control, corrective physical exercises and other healthful physical activities, are the only measures that with time and patience can restore health and strength.

LOSS OF WEIGHT MUST NOT FRIGHTEN US

Those who adopt our healthful pattern of living usually lose weight. To the overweight this is welcome. But even those who are of so-called "normal" weight or even underweight, must at first expect weight loss. The body in its effort to regain its health, has to bring about the needed detoxification and the elimination of foreign substances that have contributed to a breakdown of the joints. This usually causes a weight loss. The toxins must be cleaned out and the body's chemistry rebuilt. Ultimately, the weight stabilizes, and with time those who are underweight will gradually begin to gain, while those who have been overweight will establish what should be a normal weight pattern. No one can really gain too much weight by following our program because our aim is to restore the body to a healthy condition, and this means eating the right kinds of food in moderate amounts.

WHEN UNEXPECTED PAINS SHOW UP

Some pains, except when caused by overwork or stress, may often occur when the body is in the process of eliminating toxins. Carelessness with diet, or chilling may also bring them on and weather changes may remind the sufferer from time to time that he still has arthritis.

When these pains show up, what is needed is an abundance of sleep, rest and warmth. Take the comfortably hot epsom salt baths and be careful what food you eat, making sure not to overeat. A liquid diet at such times may be beneficial.

LISTEN WHEN YOUR BODY STARTS TALKING TO YOU

An arthritis sufferer, to get well, must make many adjustments. Symptoms and reactions are the body's way of speaking and should not cause panic or fright. Consult your doctor if necessary, but make sure that the doctor on whom you rely for help is conversant with the principles outlined in this book.

DRUGS AND WITHDRAWAL SYMPTOMS

At this point it is relevant to consider a problem that sometimes arises when the use of one of the cortisone family of drugs is discontinued. Drugs often create many unforeseen problems, and withdrawal symptoms can be one of them.

We wish to reiterate the fact that if sufferers from arthritis are to get well, all drugs must be discontinued. The conventional aspirin or other commonly-prescribed pain relievers can usually be given up without too much difficulty.

When it comes to cutting out the cortisone-type drugs, however, the story is sometimes entirely different. Doctors specializing in the treatment of arthritis know how severe the withdrawal symptoms can be when these drugs are discontinued.

In our *Encyclopedia of Natural Health,* we relate the story of a woman being treated with cortisone and who, after discontinuing the use of the drug, lost all power to walk or stand, although she was not really paralyzed, it took a long time before this patient's strength and confidence were sufficiently restored to enable her to walk again.

Another case with which we had great difficulty comes to mind. This patient's joints were completely stiffened and rigid when she started our regimen and she was greatly wasted. Some joints were puffed and swollen, while others were shrivelled up. She had been living on cortisone for many years, but after we stopped the drug and started with our cure, her joints regained much of their flexibility and freedom and the swollen areas began to disappear. Her pains diminished and in general she commenced to show improvement.

There was one thing that we did not foresee. By the time she came to us for help her body had already become badly addicted to the drugs that she was taking and so—without any apparent reason—she began to complain of agonizing pains. There was no indication that her condition was in any way deteriorating. Her joints continued to be free and flexible, and none of the other physical improvements appeared to have changed. Yet the pains seemed so real and terrible that she finally returned to her old drug-taking regime. Helen R., in describing her experiences, tells how she had to break away from these drugs more gradually, and we have often wondered whether we would not have been more successful with this case had we attempted to withdraw these drugs slowly.

DIFFICULTIES OFTEN ENCOUNTERED

While the measures outlined in the preceding pages provide the only sound care for sufferers from arthritis or other rheumatic conditions, we do not wish to imply that in some cases the damage may not have progressed to the point where complete correction is no longer possible.

In some cases the bones may already have become completely fused and when this has happened, no known treatments can unlock the fully-ankylosed joints and restore flexibility or motion. In such cases it is essential that we make sure whether the presence of stiffness or rigidity is the result of a true ankylosis or whether adhesions or a thickening of the bony structures have brought about a locking of the joint or joints. When the condition is due to adhesions or a thickening of the bones, the picture is less discouraging, and care in accordance with individual requirements will often bring about desired results.

The care outlined in this book will bring about healing of the inflamed areas and promote as much repair as possible considering the degree of damage. In time, many patients will return to a useful and normal life.

Thickening, calcification and overgrowth of bones (spurs), frequently cause pressure on a nerve or nerves, and this often leads to weakness, an impairment in function, wastage of muscles, even a certain amount of paralysis. Similar difficulties can arise when softened or weakened bones bend and cause pressure on adjacent nerves and other tissues. We called attention to the fact that osteoporosis or softening of the bones with spontaneous fractures often develop from the use of cortisone or some of its other related drugs. Here is yet another warning that these drugs must be discarded.

Numbness, rigidity, loss of muscle tone, wastage of muscles and loss of power, are some of the impairments found in these cases. Where they occur there is often little or no pain, since the pressure exerted on the nerves impairs their ability to transmit the sensation of pain. Patients may actually begin to suffer new pain or feel a renewal of old ones, when their condition improves as a result of proper care.

Increased pains or renewal of old pains is often a favorable sign; it shows that the pressure on the nerves is being released, and that as a result they are again able to react to the existing irritation or pressure.

The following is a case history of one of the patients who suffered from this problem and who made remarkable progress through our care. We will let Clare R. tell her own story.

"It is hard to say just when I became aware that something was wrong. My first complaint was a buckling in the knee, now and then. It was annoying enough to see a doctor, who labelled it a kink. It really kinked up in the seventh month of my pregnancy; there was such severe pain in the right leg that I was unable to walk or sleep. This time it was diagnosed as pressure from the embryo on the sciatic nerve which could be relieved once the baby was born. Not only did this not follow, but my right arm swelled to three times its normal size, and the wrist dropped. Doctors, neurologists, were puzzled and made every conflicting diagnosis. But none could recommend treatment. A year after the baby's birth, I accidentally stumbled onto a chiropractor who gave me my first ray of hope. In two months I was sleeping normally, and in four months, walking and using my hand.

"Several years went by when I felt pain, this time in the small of my back. I couldn't locate the original chiropractor and tried many without success. Walking became laborious and, in despair, I went to medical doctors. Again, there were tests and X-rays and wild guesses, but no treatment with any success, and no relief. I tried cortisone, a shoe horn brace and then a full brace, but I was losing ground fast.

"On vacation, I met a woman who told me of her stunning success with natural health methods. I immediately contacted the doctor she recommended. I have been following the treatment for about a year. My physical body is taking on new expression. Instead of progressive muscular stiffening, the muscles are loosening and relaxing. I find myself bending with ease and flexing so easily. I exercise with much ease. I walk with less difficulty and more endurance. I can do much more work and tire less easily. But, primarily, I have a feeling of well-being. My physical appearance—skin, hair and eyes—reflect good health and glowing spirits. I am confident that I will eventually lick the physical handicap, although the ultimate result will take more time."

A specialist, examining the X-rays taken in this case some time before our care was adopted, provided the following reading: "Osteoarthritic changes—arteriosclerotic changes—scoliosis—mild osteoporosis—bones softened and compressed." He advanced the opinion that this condition could cause pressure on the nerves, leading to impairment in function and paralysis.

Commenting on this case further, we wish to say that Clare R. had been wearing a brace on her left leg for more than two years, and that her ability to walk kept on diminishing. We insisted that the brace be removed immediately. The patient followed all instructions faithfully, and improved almost from the start. The wasted muscles began to rebuild; muscular control and coordination were gradually regained, and while occasional reactions set in, she continued to make progress. This despite the fact that we could never be sure whether the pressure on the nerves could be entirely lifted, or if the existing damage could be overcome completely.

You will note that Clare R. wrote her case history after following this care for about a year. Some of this time—approximately 2½ months—she spent at our Florida Spa in Orlando, the health resort Helen R. wrote about in her story, *Paradise, Florida,* and where our program is being carried out under the supervision of doctors specializing in natural healing. Normally, patients do not have to be away from home to obtain the benefits they need. The majority of patients who have been under our care for these disorders and who recovered, received all the attention they needed at home. But where a visit to a resort is possible, it could be of added advantage.

About a year later, Clare decided to repeat her visit to the Spa. While there, she was put on a fast for six days, and during this time complete bed rest was prescribed. Some six weeks later, the patient explained that this resulted in a loss of seven pounds. "I now weigh 119 pounds," she wrote. The fast made her quite weak and her climb back to vitality took more time than on her previous visit there, but "now I am functioning beautifully. I participate in most of the exercises, sunbathe early and late afternoon with much rest in between. My leg and foot are performing quite well."

She states further, "I will be in touch with you as soon as I get back. I want you to admire the wonderful job of building up I have done."

Because the term "building up" is often misconstrued, we wish to stress that this patient did not mean building up in weight, but in strength and improved health.

We warned in a previous chapter that some of the most difficult problems often encountered in the more advanced cases of arthritis are not those that result from the disease itself, but from the drugs prescribed for its treatment. Serious complications can ensue, tending to aggravate the problem and create a certain amount of irreversible damage, limiting the improvement that could otherwise be achieved.

MECHANICAL AIDS

In certain cases of arthritis, where pains are frequently severe and excruciating, mechanical aids such as braces or casts are often employed. The iron collar around the neck, braces or casts on hips or knees, are examples of such supports. They are used to immobilize and rest the joints, and this often provides great relief from pain. In using them, however, we frequently run the danger of causing complete ankylosis, with stiffness and rigidity for life. Care along the lines indicated in this book will mostly obviate the need for mechanical aids. We have seldom found any necessity for them. Where they have to be used they should be removed as soon as possible and gentle exercises—to restore normal functioning and prevent a permanent locking of the joints— should be encouraged.

WHAT ABOUT TRACTION?

In some conditions, especially those involving the lower part of the back, such as the sacroiliac or the lumbosacral joints, traction is sometimes recommended.

This accomplishes the opposite of what is expected from mechanical aids. Supports are used to immobilize or rest a joint or group of joints, while traction is employed to stretch the body so that pressure on the nerves is relieved and spasms overcome. We approve of using general manual manipulations and gentle stretchings to loosen tensions and relieve spasms, but regard forced traction as risky and potentially harmful. Furthermore, we must always bear in mind that unless our overall program is followed carefully, no lasting results can be expected.

DOROTHY M.'s CASE HISTORY

Here is a case proving the futility of resorting to local traction or other conventional treatments, without following a carefully planned rebuilding program. We asked Dorothy M. to send us a report of her experiences and here is what she writes: "Four years ago I suffered an injury to my spine in the 3rd lumbar region. I was under the care of my chiropractor for four months, but there was no improvement. In fact, it was getting worse. I could hardly walk; sitting was torture. Sometimes I could find relief lying on the hard floor. I developed sciatica of the left leg and was in a great deal of pain.

"After using micro-waves with no success, my chiropractor (who was a personal friend), told me he could do no more for me and that I should go to an orthopedic M.D. After the doctor's examination he ordered me to the hospital where I was in traction for two weeks, which was very painful. When the weights were removed, I was worse than before. The doctor wanted to do a myelogram on me as he felt that possibly the only thing that would help me would be surgery. But, I was terrified of needles and surgery on my spine, and insisted that I wanted to go home from the hospital and think it over.

"The next day, my mother (who was a former patient of Dr. Warmbrand), called me and asked me to go and see him. I was very skeptical and went reluctantly because I could not see how diet could affect a damaged back. But I went feeling 'what is there to lose?' I could not sit, so I lay in the back seat for the two-hour trip. I'll never forget my painful walk into the office, shuffling step by step like a cripple.

"When Dr. Warmbrand examined me, he told me that if I would cooperate he would be able to help me and have me dancing some day! That sounded unbelievable! But, I figured I would give him the six months' cooperation even though I still couldn't see how fruits and vegetables would heal an 'aching back.'

"I soon learned that there was more to the treatment than diet (but now I know the importance of *that*). My bed rest, hot baths, moist heat applications, supervised exercises, plus Dr. Warmbrand's treatments, all combined to strengthen my nerves and muscles.

"It was not an overnight cure; it took time and patience and hard work, but seven months later I was dancing and still am. I still get a twinge—I know that I have a back condition which I'll have all my life, but I did not have to undergo surgery. I look younger than I did years ago, and I am now working on my feet every day from 9:30 a.m. to 9:00 p.m. If I would only relax and slow down I would feel even better. (We humans are funny. When we feel well we cheat a little—so easily forgetting how we suffered.)"

CHAPTER 12

A SERIOUS SPINAL DISORDER AND RHEUMATOID ARTHRITIS IN CHILDREN

SPONDYLITIS ANKYLOSIS OR "MARIE STRÜMPELL" SPINE

We have already mentioned that there are two major types of arthritis: rheumatoid or infectious arthritis and osteoarthritis, also known as hypertrophic arthritis or degenerative joint disease. We also stated that arthritis is one of many different types of rheumatism. It is closely related to muscular rheumatism (also known as myositis or fibrositis), and to neuritis, a painful inflammation or damage of the nerves.

Among the disorders closely allied to these diseases are some that deserve special discussion. The condition known as ankylosing spondylitis rheumatoid spondylitis, "Marie Strümpell" spine or "Van Bechterow's" disease, is one of them. In this disease the spinal column or parts of it become completely fused or ankylosed.

The condition often begins with inflammatory changes, erosions and thickening in the sacroiliac joints and over the years continues upwards, involving the entire spine. Occasionally, some areas may escape damage, but in the majority of cases all the vertebrae ultimately become ankylosed and distorted. The joints in the spinal column are primarily affected, but other parts of the body may also become involved. In some rare instances, the joints of the whole body become completely ankylosed and ossified in time.

The conventional treatment is usually aspirin for the relief of pain and if this fails to provide sufficient relief, another drug, phenylbutazone (Butazolidin, Azolid) is prescribed. With more severe pains, radiation treatment is applied. It is well known that neither drugs nor radiation treatments are of any help in checking the progress of this disease. We have seen how dangerous the drugs can be and the statement in the *Primer on Rheumatic Diseases* that "aplastic anemia, leukaemia and other malignant lesions are more common in irradiated spondylitics than in those who have not received radiotherapy," should be of interest.

RUSSELL D.'s CASE HISTORY

At this point the story of Russell D., who suffered from this terribly crippling type of arthritis and who came to us about thirty-two years ago for care, should be of interest.

An accident at the age of twenty-one left Russell with a damaged spine, which later started to cause much suffering. He consulted many doctors, but nobody seemed able to help him. Some years later, X-rays taken in a leading hospital showed, in the words of his wife, "that the cartilages between the vertebrae had petrified, leaving his lower spine completely rigid."

A change of climate was recommended, but for one reason or another it was not made.

Now let's see how Mrs. D. describes what we found when we first examined her husband:

"Dr. Max Warmbrand found upon examination that Russell's spine was like a board up to his shoulder blades." She then goes on to say that we told her this serious condition was beyond nature's power to repair but that by the laws of natural chemistry "the trouble could be arrested from further damage."

"My husband at that time was awakening during the

night and crying with pain from the neck becoming rigid,"
she continues.

Mrs. D. at that time was also under our care for a severe
nervous breakdown, anemia, and a fibroid tumor, for
which she was urged to submit to a hysterectomy, but
which she refused.

Since Russell's pains continued to get worse with time,
he finally agreed to follow the same regimen that we outlined for his wife. He kept his diet faithfully, took his sunbaths regularly and exercised daily.

The outcome?

"My husband (after starting with this program) continued to live a very active, useful life for thirty years,"
Mrs. D. writes, and then explains that when he died at the
age of nearly eighty it was from pulmonary emphysema
(because he refused to give up his heavy smoking), an illness entirely unrelated to his spinal affliction.

"The amazing thing is that his spinal column gave him no
further trouble during all these years," Mrs. D. adds.

Mrs. D. tells how this way of living has completely rebuilt her health. She never had the hysterectomy, and
now—at about eighty—she is as vital as ever—and enjoys
life!

While we stress that ossified or completely ankylosed
joints can no longer be made free and flexible, patients can
nevertheless obtain a great deal of help when they adopt a
well-integrated plan of living and care. They can be made
more comfortable and obtain appreciable relief. What is
even more important, joints that are not as yet completely
ossified can often be kept from further ankylosis, and the
process in many cases, especially if caught early enough,
may actually be reversed.

This is why those who become aware that they have the
beginning of this or any other related disorder would do
well to realize that only when they adopt a program of care
that rebuilds the overall health of the body, can they check
further inroads of the disease and correct the damage that is
still reversible. Where ankylosis in some joints is already

completely developed, it should serve as a warning that neglect or failure to provide proper care can lead only to further damage with ankylosis of joints that are still free and that can still be protected.

STILL's DISEASE

A type of rheumatoid arthritis found in children is Still's Disease. This condition can be most heartbreaking.

Throughout the years we have seen a number of these cases and from our experience we are convinced that the only treatment for them is the care we advocate. We are thinking back to a case that was brought to us a great many years ago:

A little girl, barely three years old, was completely encased in a cast that split in half to facilitate the removal of her body so that it could be washed and kept clean. The child was so haggard and pale, a really pitiful sight! She had just been removed from a hospital where very little hope was held out for her recovery.

When we saw her condition we were frightened. What could we promise the parents?. All we could say was that we would do our best. One thing we realized. If treatment in this case was continued as before, the child was doomed. On the other hand, the use of a more wholesome diet, baths or other forms of hydrotherapy, gentle manipulation, and the mild use of ultraviolet ray treatments or exposures to the natural rays of the sun, might give the child a chance to recover. We were convinced that only this could offer the help that the child needed, and decided to try it. We had no illusions about the nature of the disease, neither could we say that the type of care we offered provided a specific cure for this ailment. We have emphasized repeatedly, and wish to state again most emphatically, that there is no specific cure for these diseases. The ability to cure resides within the body of the patient, and recovery is only possible when through good care the inherent curative forces of the body are given a chance to do an effective job of rebuilding. We realized that the care received by the child until then only hampered her recovery, while the care we planned could unfold her recuperative possibilities and give her a chance to regain her health to whatever degree might be possible.

We took this child under our care, removing the cast, and placing her on a very wholesome diet. Before long, the girl began to show real signs of improvement, and it should not be necessary to say how happy we all were. The pallor started to disappear; her face commenced to show real life; her body gradually filled out, and the joints became more free and flexible. In time she was able to use her body, and slowly started to walk again. Progress continued, and in about eight months or so the child began to ride a bicycle.

We wish we could say that she continued to stay well. We are sure that she would have done so if only the parents had possessed the good sense to continue our plan of living. But the parents and grandparents, who were accustomed to the average conventional life, could not abstain from putting the child back on her former foods, and before long she became sick again. If, when this happened, the parents had been sensible enough to return to the care that helped her originally, not much damage would have been done. Learning their lesson, they would undoubtedly have been more careful in the future.

Evidently, however, they seemed unwilling to return to this program, and so they started going from doctor to doctor all over again. When they returned to us about five or six years later, it was only because, after all their search for some magic remedy, they were finally told that everything had been tried except gold injections, and this was their last option. Since the parents realized that gold injections were dangerous, they decided against it, and came running back to us.

The youngster's body was again completely crippled by the disease, but what was even worse, the right arm and the right leg were already utterly ankylosed, having been encased in casts some time before the parents returned to us.

We succeeded in rebuilding the health of this child, but there was no possibility of ever regaining motion in the fully ankylosed arm and leg.

We don't know what subsequently happened to this girl, but here we have a vivid example of how neglect or a return to former poor habits of living, can bring the disease back again.

THE STORY OF JANET

Janet, eleven years old when she was brought to us, offers another illustration of how effective our care can be. We had seen Janet about a year before but it was not until some eight or nine months later, when her condition was even worse than when we first saw her, that the parents finally decided to place her under our care. By that time the youngster's ankles, knees and wrists were badly crippled and rigid, and she was so full of pain that she had to be carried into our office. The parents told us that she had been hospitalized several years before; that she was treated by many doctors in the last few years, and that they were finally told there was no real cure for this disease. She was given cortisone for a while but because the parents were afraid of this drug, its use was discontinued. The parents were then told to carry on with aspirin; that in time some medicine might be discovered to help the child.

Janet had been in our care only three months when she began to exhibit some very gratifying changes; her pains had lessened greatly; the swellings had been considerably reduced and the joints were much more flexible and free. On her last two visits to our office, the child walked in by herself and when leaving, walked out under her own power.

We asked the mother to send us a summary of Janet's history from the onset of her illness. Here is what she writes:

"Couldn't even begin to tell of the frustrations we had to face to help Janet. Here's a list of some of the things we tried for her:

"For the first two years, Janet complained of vague pains in her legs. Pediatrician advised us not to worry unless swelling is present.

"A year later, chiropractor treated her every week for months—no definite diagnosis made. No improvement seen.

"By the end of that year, ankles swollen, feet turned out—big toe turned up. Admitted to hospital under care of orthopedic doctor on advice of pediatrician. X-rays taken— no definite diagnosis, no treatment given. Put under care of pediatrician. Blood tests given every day. Diagnosis— rheumatoid arthritis. Aspirin, 10 grs. every four hours around the clock. Child complained of chest and stomach pains. Became very depressed, cried often, would be alert one minute and then fall asleep the next. Developed high fever and was discharged on request of parents. Doctor said there was nothing that could be done but give aspirin every four hours.

"The following year, chiropractor treating her every week promises to help—no improvement seen.

"One year later, general practitioner treated her with cortisone by mouth for two weeks. Cortisone injected into swollen wrist—relief temporary.

"During the following year she was taken to three different doctors every week. Condition getting worse. The doctors would tell us there is no cure but still had us come back every week. Taken to allergy doctor—Janet treated every week—with injections for allergies—condition not improving. Referred to M.D. in physiotherapy—treated twice a week.

"Referred to general practitioner—seen by him about once a month.

"By this time Janet was tired of tests, examinations and doctor's visits. Pete (Janet's father) and I were tired running to doctors with no results and having bills amounting to one hundred dollars a month. We finally gave up trying."

Describing the changes that have taken place since the child has been started on this care, the mother reports:

"After keeping close to diet for three months:
Janet sleeps better.
Walking more.
Appears happier, less irritable.
Exercising more.
Dressing herself."

Two weeks after receiving this report, we saw Janet again and further improvements were visible.

Her shoulders, so rigid and stiff only a few months before, were by then freely movable; her hips were flexible and free, the swelling and thickening in the knees was materially lessened, and the ankles and feet once thickened and rigid—continued to get smaller. Although still somewhat handicapped, the youngster was able to walk without any help and almost entirely free of pain. You should have seen her face light up when we told her that in time she would be able to run like all other normal children. What a change for a child who only a short time back seemed completely helpless!

In a letter mailed to us about two years later the mother writes:

Dear Dr. Warmbrand,

Janet was required to have a physical examination by a local M.D. to get approval by the school board to have a tutor. After examining her, he would not give credit to the treatment she is receiving for the improvement in her condition in the past six months, and attributed it to a miracle from God. He told us to continue on the same treatment if we were satisfied.

Janet's knees seem to be getting more normal in size. Her wrists are moving a bit, even the more deformed one has movement. Pains are gradually diminishing in joints. Back pain and pain in leg muscles seem to have completely disappeared. Janet's disposition is much happier.

We are delighted in her improvement. You are the first one that has given us any hope that she will be normal.

Sincerely,
(Sgd.) Joyce A.

About six months later, Pete called to arrange an appointment for Janet, but we had already made our arrangements to leave for London to meet our English publishers, and had to postpone this appointment until our return. While talking to us, Peter was actually ecstatic: "She is walking like crazy—exercising and raising her legs at a 90 degree angle. She loves you!" he exclaimed.

When you read the mother's statement, you are likely to gain the impression that the improvements were brought on only because the child was kept on a diet. Of course this is an oversimplification. The child naturally was kept on a carefully planned diet; this is essential in any case, if rebuilding is to take place. However, she was also given hot baths daily, and was instructed to do mild exercises twice a day. Starting at first with the gentle exercises, we later prescribed more strenuous ones as the child's condition improved. She also received gentle manipulative treatments, as well as ultraviolet radiation.

In addition to manipulative and physiotherapy treatments, the child needed a carefully planned program of living, embracing the use of a corrective diet, properly regulated exercises, enough sleep and rest, as well as the helpful baths and other forms of water applications, to rebuild the circulation and induce comfort.

THE STORY OF BONNIE L.

A more recent case we wish to tell about is the one of Bonnie L. Two years ago, while traveling abroad, during our stay in London we received a telephone call from a lady living in Mexico. She told me that she had been suffering from Still's Disease since childhood, and that she never thought this illness could be overcome. But then she came across one of our books on arthritis.

"From the moment I started reading this book," she continued, "it made such good sense that I could hardly lay it down. I started following your instructions, and now I am all better." Then she told us that as soon as we returned from abroad she wanted to see us.

When we examined this lady a few weeks later, we told her that she must not fool herself into thinking she was all better. Even though she was free of practically all her pains, the earmarks of arthritis were still with her. Some of her joints were badly locked in, and we felt it might take about two years before she could say that she had actually conquered her illness. We further warned her that she must not be disappointed or discouraged when, during the curative phase, certain acute reactions, often accompanied by much pain and swelling, begin to show up. Only when this happens will she actually be able to say that she has really recovered.

Bonnie did not take what we said very seriously. She knew she felt well, and that was all there was to it. She spent several weeks with us in Connecticut, and then left for home.

Several months later we received a call from her. She was in the throes of a most severe type of reaction. All we could do was to tell her what she must do to obtain the needed relief, but then we also reminded her that we had warned her this might happen, and that she must not be frightened since intermediate reactions have to be expected. We further reminded her that we had told her it might take as long as two years before her affliction cleared up, and that she had to be prepared for it.

Now, just as we were going to press, we have received the following note from Bonnie:

Dear Max: Yes, Doctor, it took two years. We think of you often with our salads each day.

Fondly always,
(sgd.) Harold and Bonnie

CHAPTER 13

GOUT AND RHEUMATIC FEVER

WHAT DO WE KNOW ABOUT GOUT?

Gout is another disorder related to arthritis. It is a metabolic disease expressing itself in the accumulation and retention of high amounts of uric acid crystals in the affected tissues and joints of the body. It usually results from a defect in uric acid metabolism.

An acute attack of gout usually begins with an infection of the large toe, but also often involves other joints of the feet as well as the ankles, wrists and hands. It is seldom found in the spine, hips or shoulder. The joints become swollen, inflamed and tender, chills and fever often accompany the attacks, and the pains can be excruciating. Boyd, in his *Pathology for the Physician,* mentions that there has never been a more intriguing disease than gout or one with a more exciting history.* He quotes Talbott to show that this affliction has been known to exist even before the birth of Christ, and has plagued many eminent persons throughout recorded history. He further states that it would hardly be "an exaggeration to say that we know no more about the underlying lesion than did Sydenham when he wrote his classic account of the torture of an attack of gout in 1683."

Chronic gout results when the precipitated uric acid crys-

Pathology for the Physician, William Boyd. Philadelphia: Lea & Febiger, Sixth edition, 1958.

tals are deposited in the tissues and joints of the body. In some cases, small bumps or nodules (tophi), develop from the deposit of these crystals in the soft bones or cartilages of the ears. These nodules often disappear, but others form as long as the metabolic disorder continues. We remember the case of an extremely overweight young man whose fingers, hands, knees and hips were completely deformed. Each joint was enlarged to many times its normal size and many showed large ulcerations from which dry, flaky crystals kept shredding out.

The drug most often used in the treatment of this disease is colchicine. It usually aborts an acute attack, and is therefore generally chosen. It in no way restores normal metabolic functioning, nor does it help to overcome this extremely agonizing ailment.

Furthermore, it often creates serious gastrointestinal disorders. It is a poison to the liver and sometimes even kills the patient.

Other drugs are now commonly prescribed for this debilitating affliction to bring about the elimination of uric acid. They may provide temporary relief; they do not provide permanent benefits, and in the long run the disease becomes more chronic in nature.

The care in acute or chronic gout or gouty arthritis is the same as in other forms of arthritis. Since these ailments are usually the outgrowth of a metabolic disorder, the patient's metabolism must be restored to normal. In the majority of cases, this can be accomplished with a more healthful diet, sufficient rest, sleep and relaxation; also the patient must follow a well-integrated program of exercises, and discard the health-debilitating habits that are part of an average person's life. Proper emotional control must also be part of such a program.

WHERE DOES RHEUMATIC FEVER FIT IN?

Describing rheumatic fever, doctors often quote a saying ascribed to E. L. Laseque, which runs something like this: "It licks the joints and bites the heart."

Rheumatic fever primarily affects the young. It usually starts with an acute inflammation and painful swelling of the joints, and before the condition is brought under control, many of its victims are left with permanently damaged hearts. It is this later complication that often makes doctors wonder whether rheumatic fever is to be classed among the rheumatic diseases, or should be listed among the diseases of the heart.

While most cases start with painful swellings in the joints, it is well to remember that the acute inflammatory process does not always limit itself to the joints. The heart, the blood vessels, the kidneys, the nerves, as well as other organs of the body are often involved, while occasionally the joints are free and clear.

Chorea, or St. Vitus Dance, an acute rheumatic inflammation affecting the nerves, is a variation of this disease.

One can easily understand why parents are frightened when rheumatic fever, in one form or another, strikes at their children. They know that, as a rule, these cases take a long time to mend, and that the illness often returns even after the patient has apparently recovered. Furthermore, they are never sure whether their child's heart may not remain crippled for life.

What we would like to stress, and what it is important that parents understand, is that while rheumatic fever is not a disease that can be neglected, it is not as dangerous as it seems; when treated correctly, it will, in most cases, leave no blemish or mark of any sort on the heart or on any other organ of the body. Nor does the disease have to recur!

Rheumatic fever is frightening not because it is difficult to overcome, but because the care normally provided often fails to help the body in its effort to conquer the diseased condition.

The conventional remedy in rheumatic fever is aspirin, or what is technically known as acetylsalicilic acid, and here is the villain. We know that aspirin can suppress the inflammatory process of rheumatic fever and relieve pain, but it does not in any way help to bring about correction, and many doctors are beginning to realize that the use of this drug can lead to severe and often crippling side-effects.

In reality, its use directly or indirectly, can contribute to the development of a permanently damaged heart.

In one of our former discussions of this frightening disease we referred to Dr. Paul Dudley White who, although explaining that in its treatment, aspirin is the drug of choice, nevertheless pointed out that prolonged use of aspirin "may depress the production rate of immune bodies in the organism" and mask "the persistent activity of the rheumatic infection"—in other words, actually interfere with the body's defenses!

Dr. White also stated: "It is of considerable importance to recognize that evidence of the persistent activity of the rheumatic infection may be masked by the long-continued use of salicylates, which abolishes temporary symptoms and signs including fever and leukocytosis."

In a previous section of this book we referred to Krassnoff and Bernstein, who explained how dangerous this drug can be. These authors, too, did not mince any words when they affirmed that aspirin has a toxic effect "on the central nervous system, the cardiorespiratory system and gastrointestinal system," as well as the liver, the kidneys and the skin.

Now what is the treatment that can combat rheumatic fever most effectively and can help to protect the body against recurrences as well as against possible heart damage? The first need is complete bed rest. All doctors recognize that these patients need complete bed rest so that the powers of the body are given a chance to organize their defenses in an effort to counteract the unhealthy influences and overcome the inflammatory condition.

Then we recommend comfortably hot baths with one glassful of epsom salt added to the bath, once or twice a day. Following the hot baths, the patient is immediately returned to bed, and is well covered to induce perspiration. This promotes the elimination of toxins through the skin and kidneys, and is of great help in counteracting the disease process.

Moist, hot compresses applied to the painful and swollen joints often induce relief and provide a great deal of comfort.

We insist that the patient be kept as calm and serene as possible, and to accomplish this, we urge that visitors be kept out of the sick room during the acute stage of the illness.

Finally, we stress the need of a carefully regulated diet. We start at first with freshly squeezed fruit juices or other nourishing liquid foods or beverages such as the hot vegetable broth or one of the favorite herb teas. This is usually maintained until the temperature is brought under control, and then we begin adding more solid foods. We commence with fresh fruits, gradually add raw and steamed vegetables, baked or boiled unpeeled potatoes, and finally, moderate amounts of easily digestible protein ingredients. We make certain that all concentrated sugars and sweets, e.g. ice cream, cakes and pastries, be omitted, that no sharp condiments or spices be used, and that no processed or denatured foods be permitted.

When cared for along conventional lines, sufferers from this disease normally take a long time to recover, and no one is quite sure what the final outcome will be.

On the other hand, the care outlined in these pages provides most gratifying results, and the patient usually returns to real health much more rapidly. The fever is generally brought under control in a relatively short period of time, and when it subsides it is not because it is being suppressed, but because the toxic condition that produced it is being eliminated. The swellings of the joints and the accompanying pains begin to lessen and gradually clear up entirely. We wish to reiterate that all these improvements take place not because the disease is being suppressed, but because the diseased condition is being corrected.

The great difference between the care advocated in this book and conventional routine treatment is to be found first and foremost in the fact that all medication is normally discarded.

In doing this, we make sure not to interfere with the body's defense mechanism and to allow its defensive powers free rein to respond without any restraints to the needs and challenges of the existing situation.

Since the measures employed help to improve circulation, promote the elimination of toxins and aid in general rebuilding, it does not take long before real results begin to show up.

We make sure that patients eat only the kinds of food that provide valuable nourishment in easily digestible form. This helps them to overcome their toxic conditions and promotes recovery.

In cases where heart damage has already occurred, our program is still the only one that can rebuild the patient's health to the point where a normal life becomes possible again. In our *Encyclopedia* we present a number of case histories to illustrate how effective this regimen can be when applied from the very onset of the disease. Where heart damage has already occurred, the care is often lifesaving. The following case history, written by a successful business man, Mr. I.S., proves how valuable this approach is. Following several bouts of rheumatic fever, he was left with a badly damaged heart, together with a variety of other debilities. Here is how he describes it: "My search to recapture health was futile and I resigned myself to the idea that the medical profession was doing all that was possible and tried to accept the statement that I must learn to live with my condition.

"I was a desperate victim of maltreatment, sick of being sick, frustrated spiritually and physically, financially down, tired, worn, sad and weary.

"Just when hope and despair was at its lowest point, 'destiny' favored me in a fortunate meeting with Dr. Max Warmbrand, who brought me back into the land of truly living.

"To Dr. Max Warmbrand I owe a great debt of gratitude for his kind and patient understanding and gentle guidance which helped me back on the road to recovered health and sane, sensible and rational living.

"Dr. Warmbrand's knowledge of the laws of life; his forthright advice on the issues of health by natural treatment; his answers to many disturbing questions on why nature's way succeeds where medicine fails; his all encompassing knowledge and background in nutritional research combined with his long years of experience in the prevention of disease, served as a guide and inspiration for me.

"Adherence to Dr. Warmbrand's health program not only added years to my life, but more important, it added productivity and vitality to my years.

"Attesting, and as proof of my regeneration, in the year of 1935, not a single insurance company would write a standard policy on my life—ten years later, thanks to Dr. Warmbrand's supervision and care, three major insurance companies issued standard policies on my life in upward of six figure amounts."

This case history, like the many others presented in this book, must not be looked upon as a testimonial to the author; it is in reality, evidence of a way of living and care that can erase hopelessness and disease and build a new, creative life when followed consistently and painstakingly.

We stressed on many occasions in the past and wish to repeat once more, that we have no miracle drugs; we offer no remedies or nostrums that in some magic way can restore the health of the sick. All we do is teach a clean and healthy way of living, and those who are fortunate enough to encounter this new regimen while still well, and make use of this knowledge intelligently, can be assured of staying healthy through life. On the other hand, those whose health has already broken down and who, because of previous failures, have reached the point of hopelessness and despair, should consider finding this new approach a blessing; it offers the only sure road to renewed and healthy life.

While Mr. I.S.'s response to our methods proved particularly striking—almost miraculous—it is advisable to repeat that the program offers no specific cure for any disease, and this holds true with regard to rheumatic fever or acute inflammatory rheumatism; rheumatic heart disease, or for that matter any type of heart trouble. It is essential to bear in mind that not all cases are alike, and we can never be sure whether in certain instances the damage to the heart may not have progressed to the point where complete repair is no longer possible. The treatment we present in this book provides help, not because it offers a specific cure for rheumatic fever or rheumatic heart disease, but because the health of the whole body is strengthened and rebuilt, and this in turn promotes all possible healing and renovation.

One other point needs repeating, lest we have failed to make it sufficiently clear before. Since rheumatic fever patients need experienced guidance, one should whenever possible endeavor to obtain skilled professional help. It is essential, however, that the doctor who is consulted at such times be fully conversant with the principles outlined in this book, and that he possess the necessary experience to apply them.

CHAPTER 14

OTHER RELATED DISORDERS

WHAT CAN WE DO FOR BURSITIS?

Bursitis is another disorder closely related to arthritis. The bursa is a sac containing a viscid fluid serving to protect the joint against friction. Bursitis originates from an internal toxic disorder, or may be caused by strain or injury.

As an illustration of how quickly an acute attack can be overcome, we asked Mrs. Marian A. to tell us how she went about correcting this condition when she experienced it. Here is a copy of the letter she sent us:

Dear Dr. Warmbrand:

Perhaps you will recall that attack of acute bursitis in my shoulder and arm. I remember that the pain was so excruciating that my sister could not get me dressed, and she had to take me to your office in a nightgown and coat.

Perhaps you can recall that you prescribed hot epsom salt baths and no drugs. I remember that after getting in and out of the first bath—a process so agonizing that I shrieked with pain—my sister called you to say that I insisted on a drug. Your answer was a loud and unequivocal "no." You did say that after enough of the hot baths, I would be relieved.

Well, Dr. Warmbrand, that day I took seven or eight hot baths. While in the tub, I got some measure of relief, but between baths the pains were very bad.

I did start to notice, however, after having taken three or four baths, that in the intervals between baths the pain was not quite so severe, and that I was able to remain out of the baths for increasingly longer intervals.

After about the seventh or eighth bath, the pain diminished to a point where I fell asleep—without pain—and slept for six hours or so. When I awakened, the pain had returned, but to a markedly lessened degree, and I was able to take the fresh citrus fruit juice. That day, I continued my hot epsom salt baths. By the evening I felt like a different person! I didn't even feel weak. Nor did I have the drug "hangover" which I had had in the past after using drugs. It was almost as if I had had an internal housecleaning.

Thank you from the bottom of my heart.

Ever gratefully,
Mrs. Marian H. A.

In connection with Mrs. A's case, we wish to say that this happened many years ago, and that at no time since then has there been a recurrence of her condition. Of course, Mrs. A. is adhering to a careful program of living. She eats only wholesome, natural foods, and recently told us this regimen benefits her not only physically, but is also enjoyable.

SIMPLE, NATURAL CARE MOST EFFECTIVE IN ACUTE BURSITIS

While the pains in acute bursitis can be most excruciating, effective and quick relief can usually be obtained, not through drugs, but through natural care.

Drugs must be shunned because they merely mask an acute attack and leave the joints greatly weakened and subject to chronic bursitis with deposits of calcium.

Abstinence from solid food for a day or two, followed by a carefully regulated diet, plenty of rest and sleep, and the application of moist, local heat, plus complete rest to the affected joint, normally helps to overcome an acute bursitis attack within a few days.

In acute bursitis of the shoulder, the application of heat locally and the use of a sling to provide complete rest to the shoulder joint, is of great importance. After the acute pains are overcome, gentle stretching exercises are recommended to prevent the development of a permanently locked shoulder joint. The first exercise for the damaged shoulder joint is to start climbing up and down the wall with the fingers of the affected side. Place your hand on the wall, and with your fingers keep climbing upwards as far as you can reach. Do this two to three times daily, and each time try to reach a little higher. This stretches the arm and loosens up the locked joint.

It is essential to realize that unless an acute attack of bursitis is cared for in this simple, natural way and is then followed by a healthful manner of living, it is likely to recur and in time grow into a chronic bursitis. This means deposits of calcium, adhesions and persistent, agonizing pains.

CARE ESSENTIAL IN CHRONIC BURSITIS

Once the chronic condition has been permitted to develop, prolonged care in accordance with our principles becomes essential.

We remember when Mollie B., a woman in her thirties, came to us for help because of chronic arthritis in one of her shoulder joints. Calcium had already accumulated in the joint, causing it to become thickened, or locked in, and for some time she had taken pain suppressants and other antiarthritic remedies, but to no avail.

Finally, the doctor who was treating her, told her that the only alternative he could suggest was an operation to scrape away the calcium from the diseased joint. The patient was not sure that this would make her well, so she placed herself, instead, in our care. About a year later, when she was re-examined by her former doctor at the same hospital, to his amazement, and to the amazement of several of his colleagues, new X-rays showed that the calcium deposits evident in the X-rays taken about a year or so before were no longer there. The patient reported to us that the doctors seemed greatly baffled.

SLIPPED OR HERNIATED DISCS

The articular discs between the spinal vertebrae are composed of semi-soft cartilagenous tissue. They cushion the joints and protect them against friction and injury, acting as shock absorbers. These discs, especially those in the lower parts of the spinal column, are particularly prone to strain and injury, and this often causes a great deal of pain and suffering. Calcium deposits frequently accumulate in these joints, only intensifying the suffering.

In such cases the pains are commonly unbearable, and when they persist without any hope of relief, surgery is often recommended to remove the injured part, or to bring about fusion of the joint. These operations are risky and can leave the body permanently crippled. It should be apparent that the best way to counteract this disorder is to eliminate friction as much as possible, and then attempt to repair the existing damage through good care and a healthful way of living. These cases require plentiful rest, the application of heat, a carefully regulated diet, and sometimes some mechanical supports, especially during the severely acute attacks.

The following case history, written by a well-known dental authority and educator, explains how effective this type of care can be. Before adopting our regimen, the doctors who treated him diagnosed a herniated disc condition.

"About fifteen years ago I developed low back pains. This was attributed to my occupation. The pain would last for two or three weeks, then disappear for two or three years.

"Two years ago, following some strenuous golf, I developed severe low-back pain which radiated to my right leg. I consulted an orthopod who tested my reflexes and advised a support. The pain got worse; I consulted a second orthopod who recommended surgery. I went to a third one who suggested novocaine injections, and exercises if the pain disappeared. Months went by and the pain became worse. I also went to a chiropractor and an osteopath.

"After eight months of wandering I consulted a fourth orthopod and I asked to be hospitalized. He placed me in traction for two weeks. I improved a little so he dismissed me. After a month the pain was severe—my back was rigid.

"I consulted a fifth orthopod who suggested six weeks of complete bed rest. I followed his advice and improved tremendously. The pain was gone but I was weak.

"I returned to work and rested every hour for fifteen minutes. Rest seemed to be the best treatment.

"After a month I noticed the pain began to return. At this point I consulted a naturopath. He recommended a natural diet, rest and manipulation. I followed this carefully for eight months. My back improved greatly, although I lost 1/7 of my total body weight. I felt good and vigorous. My back was not painful as long as I did not fatigue myself. There is no question that this new way of life is beneficial to general health and well-being.

"This summer I played a mild game of golf. I am still cautious about my back and find that I must not fatigue myself. I hope that as I continue this regimen my back will continue to improve so that I can follow a normal, vigorous and active life."

This doctor, holding a professorship in one of the leading dental universities, had no difficulty in obtaining the care he thought he needed, and while he did achieve periodic relief, it was only when he adopted the overall care that we advocate in this book, that he succeeded in really regaining his health.

The doctor is now fully aware of the importance of a carefully regulated diet; he is continuing with his hot epsom salt baths, adhering to a carefully planned program of exercises, and is obtaining as much rest as possible.

While doctors diagnosed his case as a herniated disc condition, it is well to point out that not all of these agonizing back conditions are caused by true disc damage. Calcium deposits settling in and around the joint areas, can create enough pain even though no true disc injury exists. All who suffer from excruciating back pain, whether the result of a true disc involvement or not, must adopt our care if they are to obtain real help. And we must remember that we treat a person, not a disease, and that the care in all forms of arthritis or rheumatism, whether called by one name or another, must be adapted to the needs of the individual case. As we pointed out on several occasions, these patients should, whenever possible, receive expert guidance, but the care they obtain must conform to our program.

LUMBAGO

The term lumbago covers a multitude of disorders and is not necessarily limited to the simple backache. Backaches often show up in connection with arthritis, muscular rheumatism, weakened back muscles, or neuritis, or may occur in conjunction with various internal disorders. Prolapsed organs, intestinal ailments, pelvic diseases, prostatitis, growths, often cause "referred" back pains.

The application of heat and hot baths, exercises, and a properly planned dietary program are of great help in these cases. To obtain lasting results, however, the disorders that have contributed to the onset of backaches must receive the necessary care. Where skilled professional help is available, the right type of manipulative treatment, ultraviolet radiation, as well as other carefully selected physiotherapy treatments, can be of added help.

PAGET'S DISEASE OF THE BONE

Paget's Disease is another of the many arthritis-related disorders. In the early stages the bones become decalcified and softened but later they become thickened, bent and deformed. In this disease, the bones of the legs, the arms, the spine, the pelvis and the head are often affected, although other bones may be involved. The ailment is a disturbance of bone metabolism, and care for it is essentially the same as for arthritis. A change to wholesome, natural foods, plenty of rest and sleep, proper emotional control, hot epsom salt baths, carefully regulated exercises, the elimination of all health-devitalizing habits, plus all other care suggested in this book, must be consistently followed if beneficial results are to be obtained.

CHAPTER 15

DRUGS—A REAL HAZARD
TO HEALTH

We cannot reiterate too strongly the fact that pain is nature's warning that something is wrong. The body is crying out for help, and when drugs or other suppressive remedies are employed, they merely stop the body's warning cries, but do not rebuild health. When these acute reactions occur, the temptation is often great to turn again to the pain-relieving drugs. However, it is essential to bear in mind that every time we permit ourselves to be swayed from our course and return to their use, we only interfere with the body's endeavor to bring about correction, thereby causing more destruction and greater suffering. This also explains why some patients become addicts for life, and why their chances for recovery are often lost forever.

The patient who starts out on this new regimen must understand that it is the beginning of a new kind of life. The start may not always be easy. When the pains, or the acute symptoms that have been blocked out by some of the suppressive remedies begin to reawaken, the patient can easily be led astray. It is at such times that worry takes over, and the sufferer begins to wonder whether his condition is not really getting worse. It is then that a great deal of courage and determination are required. *The patient must realize that only when he follows a program of care that rebuilds the health of the whole body, can he obtain lasting results.* It is at such times that the services of a doctor who is conversant with the principles explained in this book can be of great help, because he can indicate what is actually taking place and provide the necessary encouragement and guidance.

SEARCH FOR A SPECIFIC REMEDY FALLACIOUS

People have been trained to look for specific remedies, and even those who realize that potent drugs are injurious and must therefore be avoided, often wonder whether some preparation which otherwise could be nondamaging to the body, might not possess certain definitely curative qualities that would be of help in their case.

Recently we were told of a man who suffered severely from chronic arthritis, and who, by taking an infusion made of alfalfa seeds, succeeded in eliminating his pains completely. He took five to six teaspoonfuls of alfalfa seeds and soaked them for six to eight hours in a quart of warm water. He then brought them to the boil and kept them boiling under a low flame for about fifteen minutes. After letting the mixture cool off, he took three to four glasses daily for several weeks, and this provided the looked-for relief.

Every so often we hear of some remedy that performs wonders. But how long do these miracles last? We have no reason to doubt that this man felt better after taking the infusion, but we must never begin to think that simply because the use of a certain herb or seed is followed by improvement, that it possesses specific curative powers. It is well known that even placebos (make-believe drugs) provide significant relief in a great many cases. In this particular instance, since alfalfa seeds are a food, and rich in vitamins, minerals, trace elements, as well as other valuable nutrient substances, an infusion made from them could be beneficial.

We advocate the use of tasty, natural herb teas and wholesome foods, not because they possess definite healing powers, but because they are rich in vital, protective food substances. All cure emanates from within the body and good food and healthful care merely supply the body with what it needs so that it can function more effectively, to enable it to bring about the necessary repair and renovation.

We must always remember that the power of healing is one that is inherent in the living organism, and that this power functions most efficiently only when favorable conditions for repair and rebuilding are established. Our task is to make certain that these conditions are created and maintained so that the body can function at its best. This is the only way that real help can be attained.

IT TAKES TIME TO GET WELL!

Furthermore, we must remember that it takes time to get well! It takes years to undermine the health of the body, and we only fool ourselves when we think that some magic drug, special gadget, or even a miracle food, can take the place of over-all good care and healthful living habits. Years of abuse cannot be rectified in a few weeks! Unless we understand this fully and have the patience and perseverance to follow through, no lasting results can be expected.

CHAPTER 16

A PLAN THAT SUCCEEDS

The case histories that we present illustrate what the sufferer from arthritis, or one of its other related ills, can accomplish when the measures outlined in this book are conscientiously applied and consistently followed.

These case histories represent but a few of countless thousands of people who, by adopting this plan of living and care, succeed in regaining their health.

We emphasize that these patients should whenever possible obtain skilled professional guidance. However, what should those do who, for one reason or another, are unable to obtain this kind of help; are they doomed to a life of misery and suffering?

By no means, if they are willing to apply themselves with determination to the program presented in this book and are resolved to persevere with it, making proper allowances for individual needs and adjustments.

To illustrate what we mean, we would like to reproduce a letter which Fred Allen, famous humorist and radio entertainer, received some years ago. He forwarded it to us at a later date.

Mr. Fred Allen
New York City, N.Y.

Dear Fred:

Some time ago my sister-in-law, Miss Irene Schlegel, wrote you, thinking that you had been cured of arthritis, and she wanted to know what the treatment was that you had used. You replied that you had never had arthritis but that you were *requesting a publisher to send me a book on the treatment of this disease.*

I have been suffering for almost two years and now have tried everything.

At the time my sister-in-law wrote you, I couldn't even hold a pen in my hand, I was in such a condition. I want to take *this opportunity of telling you how grateful I am to you for having this book, by Max Warmbrand,* sent to me. Since receiving it I have followed it faithfully with the exception of taking treatments from a physiotherapist and the only reason I didn't do that was because I haven't been able to get one to take my case. Regardless of this fact, I am getting along fine and am *improved so much,* that I have been *back to work now for the past two* months and yesterday I was able to *plant grass seed on our lawn.* I was in such a bad condition last December that my *wife had to dress me* and *even feed me at times,* so when I tell you that I am so very thankful to you for your kind interest, it is putting it mildly.

Very gratefully yours,
(Sgd.) A.P.

(Incidentally, it was Fred Allen who, for the sake of emphasis, underlined certain portions of this letter before he mailed it to us.)

Another letter illustrating what a person can do who is really determined to get well, is the one we received from Mrs. H.H.W. This is what this remarkable seventy-nine-year-old lady writes:

Dear Dr. Warmbrand:

Yesterday, in looking up a telephone number, I ran across your name in the directory, and I am wondering if you are the author of the book, *New Hope for Arthritis Sufferers.* If so, I would like to ask you whether you place fish in the same category as meat in outlining your diet.

Assuming that you are the author of this very valuable

book, you may be interested to know that a year ago last July, I was practically ossified after many years of arthritis, although I had spent thousands of dollars in treatments by the most eminent doctors. My joints are again free and I am almost entirely cured after faithfully following the regimen you laid down.

I am really a "museum piece" to confirm your theory. I might add that my daughter ran across the book while browsing around in a bookstore and brought it home to me in the faint hope that I might find some relief if I followed the diet. My doctor in Washington (my winter home), said he approved of my trying it as he had done all that modern medical science knows about, without permanent relief. As I am nearly seventy-nine years old, I feel that my cure has been really phenomenal.

With thanks,
(Sgd.) Mrs. H. H. W.

The book referred to in this lady's letter, as well as the book that Fred Allen ordered to be sent to Mr. A.P., sold tens of thousands of copies, and countless letters attested to the benefits that were derived from it by people who followed our suggestions. The best of it is included here.

We have another report, this one from South Africa. Mrs. Veronica K. tells how she has been helped:

Cape Province
South Africa
3rd July, 1975

Dear Dr. Max,

Firstly, I do hope this letter reaches you as I feel that I must let you know how wonderful your book on arthritis is.

I'll start at the beginning. For the past 4 years I have been an Osteo-Arthritis sufferer. I am 47 years of age. In all this time no Medical Doctor has ever told me that there is a cure for arthritis. They only prescribed Brufen to start with and when that doesn't help anymore, something stronger. I was also told that I'd use pills till the end of my life, which I accepted. About 4 months ago I accidentally came across your book in our local library which I immediately took out. After reading only about 10 pages I realized that I must immediately follow your advice. I stopped the Brufen and dieted for 1 day on water only. The next day one kind of fruit and the day after another and the next day still another. After 4 days I found that all my pains were gone. The knees and lower back being the most affected parts. The swelling of my knees has gone back to normal. I found that for the first time after 4 years I could sit on my haunches. Needless to say I've tried to keep to your advice by eating healthily. Every week on a Monday I diet and drink only water and the next day only fruit and I find that I am entirely without pains. . . . I also lost 16 lbs. in weight about which I am very pleased. My general health is just wonderful. I now weigh 136 lbs.

Dr. Max as far as I'm concerned, by following your advice—my arthritis is healed completely.

Gratefully,
(Sgd.) Veronica K.

In reprinting these letters we do not wish to imply that those who suffer from this crippling disease should not, whenever possible, avail themselves of sound professional care. Throughout this book, we keep stressing the benefits that can be derived when the *right kind* of professional help is obtained. It should be gratifying to know, however, that even when the sufferer is not in a position, or finds it impossible, to obtain such help, much can still be accomplished when the measures outlined in this book are carefully followed.

Since conventional remedies offer nothing of any positive value to those who suffer from crippling arthritis, it is understandable why so many have come to believe that it is a hopeless and incurable disease.

Those, however, who had the courage to discard conventional practices and who adopted our care, proved to themselves and to all those who knew them, that there is no need for despair, that if they are willing and determined to follow the right path, they *can overcome their disease.*

This does not mean that joints already eroded or eaten away, or tissues that have already become utterly destroyed, can again be completely restored. It does mean, however, that even where a great deal of destruction has taken place, the right kind of care, consistently and persistently applied, can still provide much help, and bring about significant improvement to make life comfortable and pleasant.

At this point it is also appropriate that we sound a warning. Many, even among those who suffered most severely, often forget how much they have been through and tend to drift back to some of their former unhealthy habits of living. There is where danger lies. To get well we have to change to a really healthful routine, and if we are to continue to stay well this regimen must become a lifetime habit. Our life and our health should be valuable enough to us, and of sufficient importance, to make us determined to do what is best for us. We must always remember that when we return to our former careless habits of living, we are only inviting a return of our previous ailments, or encouraging the development of new ones.

CHAPTER 17

A WAY OF LIFE—
MANY HIDDEN BENEFITS

Arthritis is a crippling and extremely painful disease, and even those who are not yet suffering from it should realize that they are not immune unless they take proper precautions by adhering to a sound way of living. Furthermore, practically every family has somebody who is already suffering from this, or one of its related ailments, and therefore, all of us should be interested in finding out what can be done to overcome these afflictions—or how they can be avoided!

When in your early 20s or 30s, you hear a creaking or cracking of the joints, or when you suffer from occasional twinges of pain, or have a feeling of numbness or stiffness, do not disregard these warnings—they are the early signs of what is already developing; they are telling you that arthritis or one of its allied diseases is already making inroads.

These signs must not be neglected or disregarded if we are to protect ourselves against further deterioration and possible crippling.

THE VALUE OF A PERMANENT CHANGE

A point that is sometimes difficult to pass on is that the program presented in this book is not to be followed merely until the sufferer gets well. It has to become a way of life! It should be clear that the reason the patient is being helped is because he is following a physiologically correct way of living, and he should realize that only when this regimen is continued, can health be maintained.

Some patients tend to become restless or impatient and then sometimes drift back to their old habits of living. This happens especially when they begin to feel better. "Now that I feel fit, why can't I have a cup of coffee, a pastry, an ice-cream soda, or even a cocktail occasionally?"—is a very common plea. With some, the old habits are deeply ingrained, and they begin to reassert themselves as soon as pains lessen, while others resent having to be different. Still others feel awkward or embarrassed when they try to adopt a way of life so much at variance with the habits of their neighbors. Since time immemorial, the person who dared to think or act differently has been subject to criticism or ridicule. It takes a courageous person, or one in pain, to dare and to persist!

We know that surroundings, environment, influences and habits can lead us astray. But, we must never forget that cause and effect are ever operating. We must always remember that only when we treat our body kindly, can we keep it in a healthy condition. On the other hand, when we abuse it, the penalty we have to pay keeps growing greater with time.

MANY HIDDEN BENEFITS

The patient who adopts this wholesome health-regenerating plan of living, derives infinite benefits from it. Not only does it help to counteract the particular rheumatic disorder; it also safeguards the body against various other chronic and degenerative ills such as heart disease, hardening of the arteries, diabetes, kidney and liver diseases—scourges that take a frightful toll of human life. Furthermore, it presents us with a great many other unexpected gifts. Women are amazed at their renewed youthfulness and improved appearance. Clearer, smoother skin, sparkling eyes, lustrous hair, are some of the hidden benefits that they derive from this new, healthful way of living, while men begin to note how much more strength and vitality they gain from it. Youthfulness, beauty, renewed strength and health, are some of the hidden bonuses that often are derived from the change.

Of course, it takes time. These improvements do not always show up immediately, and sometimes are limited by the permanent changes wrought by the disease itself, as well as by the effects of previous suppressive treatments. But the potentials for benefit, when we persist and persevere, are infinite! As we continue with our dependence on wholesome, natural foods and obtain the care we need, the general health of the body is rebuilt. This is reflected in an improvement in the health of all its tissues and organs.

MRS. C's STORY

The story of Mrs. C. vividly illustrates this point.

"I see nails! Your nails are growing! What have you been doing to get them to grow?" the beautician exclaimed. She had noticed how well Mrs. C. was improving, but she became particularly interested when Mrs. C.'s nails—which until then were splitting, peeling, but not growing—suddenly began to grow again.

Mrs. C. had been suffering from arthritis for a great many years and during all this time tried practically everything suggested to her in an effort to get well. Gold injections, cortisone and a great many other drugs were prescribed for her, but none of them provided any lasting benefit. She would obtain occasional periods of relief, but there was no improvement, and as time went by, she became more severely crippled.

In recent weeks however, people began to notice how well she looked, and the beautician was particularly struck by the discernible growth of Mrs. C.'s nails.

"It's those d . . . vegetables that this doctor has been making me eat," Mrs. C. replied with a smile.

Mrs. C. never ate vegetables in all her life—actually she hated them! But we insisted that this is what she had to eat, and grudgingly she went along with us. She also followed all the other instructions that we gave her, and now she is happy because she is beginning to see how it pays off in better health and well-being.

In reality, we don't know whether this lady would have persevered—to swallow a pill was so much easier! We are not sure she really had a full grasp of what we tried to accomplish, and if it had not been for her husband's encouragement, she might never have persisted.

But her husband realized what we were trying to do, and he was there, constantly helping, encouraging, making her realize how important it was that she carry on. Results began to show before very long. The pains began to lessen. The lady started to regain her strength, she was able to stand up straighter, and her health improved in a great many ways.

When Mrs. C. came to us, her disfigured nails, their brittleness and their failure to grow, were her least concern; she never even mentioned them to us. It was the pains, the anguish, the crippling, that made her come, hoping that by adopting our plan of living and by following our suggestions she could obtain the help she needed.

The change in her nails was merely an added gift, a bonus on top of all the other benefits she derived.

One day we complimented the lady. We told her how much healthier, straighter and taller she was—she actually looked inches taller!

"Why shouldn't I? Those d . . . vegetables that you make me eat removed lumps of fat from my back and make it possible for me to stand up much straighter," she countered. Evidently the plan of living that she is now following, and the care that she is now getting, did not only start her nails growing, it actually is making an entirely new person out of her.

Recently she told us of another gain. Since she became sick, her eyelashes had fallen out and never grew back, but now they have grown in again—and they are so beautiful that people are beginning to comment on them. Her hair too, has become more alive and has become the focus of attention. Her husband told us of another one of her gains. He is an optician by profession and, for the last three years, he had his wife checked regularly for glaucoma, another condition which we never discussed before. The most recent checkup with an instrument that registers by graph the exact pressure in the eyes, disclosed such vast improvement that it was beyond the understanding of the specialist who examined her.

CHAPTER 18

HEALTH BECKONS

We can well understand why so many of those who suffer from arthritis or one of its allied diseases, feel despondent and hopeless. These ailments are little understood, and the conventional type of treatment offers very little except temporary relief. When pains continue to recur with ever greater frequency and intensity over the years, or when the joints or other involved parts of the body continue to show ever-increasing signs of deterioration, the sufferer can hardly be blamed when he begins to wonder whether there really is any help for him. However, the case histories presented above, as well as thousands of others with similar experiences, can attest to the fact that in the majority of cases, victims of arthritis *do get well*, provided they are willing to divorce themselves from conventional procedures and prejudices, and adopt this completely new approach.

In reading the case histories presented in this book, you will note that each one portrays a different picture and describes a different set of experiences. The time it took these patients to recover also varied considerably, as the case histories in the first chapter will bear out. Similar variations could be listed in the other cases.

We are bringing up these facts because it is essential that arthritis victims do not assume that all they have to do is wave a magic wand and presto—they regain health! The time it takes to recover depends upon a great many factors:

The degree of damage, the complications that often develop from the use of drugs, and the general state of health when care is started—these as well as various other considerations determine how long it takes to bring about correction. Intelligence and patience are requisites if results are to be obtained.

It must be remembered, that in some of the more advanced cases, the damage may be too far along to allow for complete restoration. We stressed before that it would be folly to assume that a joint, or joints, which have already become completely and permanently fused (ankylosed) can regain motion. It would also be fallacious to assume that complete regeneration can be achieved where the cartilage or the synovial linings, or any of the other involved tissues have already become so badly damaged that they are beyond repair.

We must never forget that normally, neither arthritis nor any of the other rheumatic diseases, stands alone. They are derangements that develop when a disturbance in the general health of the body brings about a breakdown in the functions and health of the joints or other involved tissues. This explains why the health of the whole body must be rebuilt if real correction is to be brought about. We intimated before that, in some cases, accidents such as overstrain, a fall or an injury, may cause local joint damage. However, even in these instances, good care hastens the healing of the injury and overcomes the weakness which would otherwise remain and—if not corrected—would leave a weakened and sensitive area predisposed to later breakdown.

The care we stress in these pages relates to our mode of living and takes in the various influences that affect our general health and well-being. The use of unwholesome foods, a lack of sufficient rest and sleep, the tensions that surround us, as well as other debilitating influences, impair the health of the individual, and contribute to the onset of disease.

The doctor who understands this will inspire his patients to change to a wholesome, healthful way of living, and encourage the use of sound physiological measures of care. He knows this is the only way sufferers can regain their health, and does everything within his power to further the understanding of the need for these changes. He is also of great help when—during periods of acute reactions—uncertainty and fear rear their ugly heads, creating the need for encouragement and sympathy.

We wish to repeat that we are not offering a magic drug, a miracle cure; time and a great deal of patience and determination are required. We appreciate that many changes must be made, and that some of them may test the will and endurance of the patient, particularly, as is often the case, when convention-bound friends and relatives interfere. However, if you are truly interested in regaining your health and really wish to get well, you will not shrink from the task that confronts you, since all the sacrifices that are asked of you are but minimal compared to the benefits to be derived.

Remember that science has not yet reached the point where it can create new life; it can only teach us how to preserve it, strengthen it, or rebuild it. The laboratory may claim much for its ability to analyze or explain the various elements that make up life, but it cannot in any way duplicate what the power within us can accomplish when we make sure to provide our bodies with the right kind of care. To build life and maintain it at its best is still the prerogative of nature; we must merely make certain that we do not go contrary to its laws.

We quote the poem by Joyce Kilmer: "Poems are made by fools like me, but only God can make a tree!" We wish to paraphrase this by saying that drugs can be taken by fools like thee and me, but true and lasting health can only be restored through the living, throbbing power within us. Pills and potions can suppress pain or other symptoms of disease, but only our own healing powers can build real and lasting health.

Let us therefore open our arms and hearts to nature's way, for only when we allow these powers to do their work, and when we make certain not to interfere with, but conform to, the natural laws of living, can we be confident of building renewed health and vigor!

CHAPTER 19

SURGERY IN ARTHRITIS

While the conventional treatment of arthritis is usually based on the use of a variety of antiarthritic remedies— such as cortisone, prednisone, gold injections, butazolidin, indocin, and a variety of other pain-relieving drugs including aspirin—orthopedic surgery is recommended in the treatment of certain types of arthritis.

A surgical procedure performed with success on patients whose joints have already badly deteriorated is known as orthoplasty—the replacement of broken-down or degenerated joints with joints constructed out of various materials such as steel or plastic. Many of these operations are being performed routinely on hip joints, and similar operations are recommended for badly-damaged knees, crippled shoulders and broken-down ankles.

Dr. Peter Kaklish, a well-known orthopedic surgeon connected with the Allentown, Pa. hospital, describes his hip-replacement procedure:

"In a hip operation, the neck of the thigh bone is removed to make way for a stainless steel shaft that is cemented into place as a substitute. This 'bone' is topped with a metal ball designed to move freely within a plastic socket which is cemented in to form an artificial pelvic hip socket."*

*Sunday-Call Chronicle, Allentown, Pa., February 3, 1974.

This artificial hip joint, surgically created to take the place of the patient's own hip joint, is known as a "ball-and-socket hip joint."

No one can predict the ultimate outcome of joint-replacement operations and it is well to bear in mind that they do not eradicate the disease or rebuild broken-down joints; they merely replace the patient's arthritic joint with one that has been artificially created out of steel and plastic. In the meantime, the disease progresses, and eventually more pain and crippling may result.

SEYMOUR A.'s HIP REPLACEMENT

The first postoperative orthoplastic surgical case we examined was fifty-three-year-old Seymour A., who consulted us about his arthritis problem. Mr. A. was a heavy man weighing about 230 lbs. His story was that he had never known that he was suffering from arthritis, but that after he fell down a flight of stairs, he began to experience excruciating pains. Drugs were prescribed to relieve his distress, and some time later both of his hips were replaced by artificially constructed hip joints. This, however, did not end his suffering and when he came to consult us about two years after the operations had been performed, he was in a deplorable condition. Although his hip joints had been replaced, he continued to suffer severe pains in hips and back.

He agreed to start our program, and soon after a change to better food habits and other healthful care we recommend, he noticed considerable improvement in his condition. His pains were greatly relieved; he showed a marked reduction in weight, and he became more active. He no longer depended on crutches for support.

Later this patient moved to the South and we heard that he had gradually drifted back to his former eating and living habits. As a result his severe pains returned.

Sometime after, we asked Mr. A. to tell us what had happened, and he said that when he had returned to Florida his distress had been so great that he again consulted the surgeon who had performed his first operations. The surgeon repeated the operation on the left hip and found to his amazement that during the first surgery one of the sponges had been left in the socket. The sponge was removed; the job was completed and a short time later the operation was repeated on the right hip.

Mr. A. is pleased with the results of these operations; they enabled him to return to work and to resume some of his other normal activities. But when we asked him how he was feeling otherwise, he told us that he still had a great deal of arthritic pain, but that aspirin was making it tolerable. He further stated that he hopes to return to our care, and when he said this it sounded as if he finally realized that if he were to get well, he would have to return to the regimen we originally recommended.

BETTY T.'s EXPERIENCE

Another case that comes to mind is that of fifty-two-year-old Betty T. who consulted us and said that she had been suffering from rheumatoid arthritis for many years. She was kept on prednisone, cortisone, and various other anti-arthritic drugs, but was finally urged to submit to an operation. As her husband explained it, a metal plate was inserted in her right knee, and "since the bones in both of her feet were eaten away, parts of them were also trimmed off."

These operations did not cure the patient, and her pains continued to be severe. At last she came across one of our books on arthritis and when she started with the program we suggested, she began to note a considerable amount of improvement. Mrs. T. writes, "Your program has done more for me than anything I have [tried] before." However, since we suggested a long-term program and she was unwilling to commit herself to it, she and her husband decided to go to the West Coast in the hope that the change would help her.

CHANGE OF CLIMATE NOT THE ANSWER

The idea that a change of climate can be helpful to sufferers from arthritis is not new. Many patients take periodic trips to spas and bathing resorts in the hope that it will cure them, while others hope that by moving to a warm climate they will obtain the help they need. What these sufferers fail to realize is that no matter where they go, they take their bodies and their suffering with them, although change from a less favorable climate to a more favorable climate, does provide a certain amount of relief.

HOW LILLIAN P. WAS HELPED

By contrast, let us describe how Lillian P. was helped. Lillian, too, was advised to submit to a hip-replacement operation, but she decided against it; she was told that the end results were too uncertain and in many cases, discouraging.

Lillian's arthritis, as she described it, had reached a point where every doctor who was consulted, insisted that she "would have to learn to live with the disease." She was kept on cortisone, indocin (indomemethacin), aspirin; received gold injections, and was kept on many other drugs which did not help her in any way. Meanwhile, her arthritis kept growing worse. Her joints became locked in by the calcium that settled in them, and she reached a point where she could walk only with the aid of a cane. She could sit down in a chair or get out of it, only with extreme difficulty, and getting into a car, or out of it, was a real crisis. The constriction in her arms and the pains that she felt when she moved her head prevented her from driving her car.

HIP-REPLACEMENT SURGERY SUGGESTED

Then an orthopedist, a doctor specializing in diseases of the joints, suggested a hip-replacement operation. Lillian, however, was not too keen about it. "Perhaps the operation could have been successful, but then what would happen to the rest of my joints and the continuing pains in them?"

What really made her decide against surgery, however,

was her son's insistence that she forget it. Her son, then in his last year of medical college and now an intern in a leading hospital, discussed the subject with his instructors who told him of the many uncertainties and pitfalls surrounding the operation.

LILLIAN EIGHTEEN MONTHS LATER

This was what finally brought Lillian to our office and here is how she described her recovery:

"But then the good Lord directed me to you. I listened to all you told me to do and the patients I met in your office who had already become well gave me the impetus and hope to carry on. It was very encouraging. After only three months I was without pain, and I felt myself constantly improving. After ten months I discarded the cane entirely. I have never taken any medication since I am on this program."

She continues, "The fringe benefits are great. I breathe more deeply, I have lost my post nasal drip which irritated my throat, and haven't had a cold, to which I was prone. The exercises I do have improved my circulation as well as my flexibility and my digestion improved.

"Today, after eighteen months, I do all the beautiful things I did before, and more—because I have learned how to live and take care of myself through your teachings. Thanks."

A FOLLOW-UP

Some months later, while visiting our Florida Spa in Orlando, Lillian underwent a complete physical checkup including blood tests and all other laboratory tests and, reporting on these findings, she writes: "blood pressure, normal—cholesterol, normal—and the sedimentation rate couldn't be better." She also visited her dentist who was greatly pleased with the improvement that he found in her gums and teeth.

After reporting all this, Lillian finally concludes:

"Little did I think that I would derive all these additional fringe benefits from this new way of living. And what's more, I feel ten years younger.''

LILLIAN'S LATEST REPORT

Here is another report that we received from her some months later:

"It's always nice to see you and of course one feels so much better after your treatment. I know it will make you happy to learn that for the first time in five years I walked home from the hairdresser's shop, an equivalent of eight city blocks. You can well understand my joy to be able to do so, and I had my confidence restored, because I walked alone, and mind you I felt no pain but exhilaration. Thanks again and God bless you.''

The latest we can report about Lillian is that before she became ill many years ago, she was a very active and dynamic person. Arthritis, however, made a complete invalid out of her, but this has all changed. She is again as active as in the past and is thrilled about it.

HOW GOLDIE W. IS RECOVERING

Another case, the case of fifty-five year old Goldie W. is worth telling about. Mrs. W.'s story is not much different from Lillian's except that in Goldie's case the joints were even more severely crippled and her pains were more agonizing.

Mrs. W. had been getting gold shots for about six years, but they brought on a serious blood disorder and had to be discontinued. Later, she was kept on cortisone for about a year. At first she received large doses, but when serious side-effects began to show up, the dosage was gradually decreased. For the last year of her medical care she was kept on indocin and six to eight aspirins daily.

By the time Mrs. W. visited our office her joints were already so badly crippled that every move and every step was torture. For her, getting in and out of a chair was more difficult than it had been for Lillian. We had to help her with ev-

erything. We lifted her onto the treatment table and when
we turned her from one side to another she felt very heavy
and seemed in severe pain. When we tried to move her
joints, they sounded so loud that anyone in the room, even
at the farthest end of it, could hear them. Her joints by then
were already so badly damaged that we were not certain
how much she could be helped. However, since nobody
can predict what the right kind of care can accomplish in
these cases, we decided to take on her case and see what
we could do for her.

WHY MRS. W. DECIDED AGAINST THE OPERATION

Mrs. W. too had been advised to submit to replacement
surgery. In her case, the surgeon was talking not only of replacing her hips because they were already badly broken
down, but also surgery for her knees which by then were
greatly enlarged, swollen and immobile. The doctor with
whom she discussed this type of surgery was quite frank
about it. He told her that in some cases one leg becomes
shorter than the other, and when she asked him whether her
own body might not reject the artificial replacements, his
reply was that he could not be certain. There was one other
point that made her question the advisability of submitting
to these operations. She began to realize that by cutting
away her own joints, and replacing them with artificial
joints, she was not doing anything to clear up the arthritis in
the other parts of her body. This finally made her decide
against the operations and come to us to find out what our
care could do for her.

MRS. W.'s CONDITION TEN MONTHS LATER

How was Mrs. W. ten months after she started with our
care? Here is what she had accomplished: She was still using a walker, and could walk only when she held on to
something. But she no longer had to be helped getting on
and off the treatment table, and no more did we hear any of
the creaking and cracking sounds of her joints. Sitting
down or getting up from a chair was still a problem because

her left hip was not yet altogether freely movable, but she had regained a considerable amount of flexibility and motion—much more than we had thought possible. She was also able to do a great many other things she never thought she could do again. She still had a certain amount of pain, since it takes time for spurs that cut into the flesh to flatten out or diminish in size, but the fact that her pains had diminished made her most hopeful. She looked forward to the time when she would no longer have to depend on the walker, although she knew there was a great deal of damage in her joints, and that time and patience would be required.

HIP-REPLACEMENT SURGERY SOMETIMES UNAVOIDABLE

Hip-replacement surgery is reserved for cases of extreme disability. In some rare cases and under certain conditions an operation of this kind may be unavoidable, especially when there is no other alternative or when it is the only way to restore a person to normal functioning, but to offer these operations before making sure that they are really necessary is the height of folly. Replacement devices may be understandable since they make life for many of those who need them livable again. We have mentioned before that when Mr. A. had his hip operations repeated he was able to return to work and life became livable.

SHOULDERS BUILT OUT OF STEEL AND PLASTIC

While at the time this chapter is being written, hip-replacement surgery is being performed routinely, replacement surgery for other joints has not yet been fully perfected. Nevertheless, headway is being made. We mentioned that similar operations are now being tried for badly damaged knees. The latest is shoulder-replacement surgery. "The shoulder may be the next joint for which spare parts are available," stated the *Journal of the American Medical Association* in one of its more recent reports.

Dr. Melvin Post and his colleagues, Samuel Haskell and

Irwin Carson of the Michael Reese Hospital, Chicago, have performed this operation. They describe the shoulder-replacement device as more complex than the one for hip replacement, but similar in design; it resembles the now-familiar Charnley total-hip-replacement joint, which replaces the damaged articular surfaces with a metal-to-plastic ball-and-socket joint. Dr. Post was quite honest in his statement of what he expects this operation to accomplish. He explained that it is basically "a salvage technique used only when more conservative treatment would be futile." His remark, when the press reported that the operation restored a full range of motion to the badly damaged shoulders, was sharp and to the point. "This is nonsense," he said, "it won't give back motion the patient did not have before. What it will do is give the patient a competent pain-free joint with enough mobility to perform duties that were painful or impossible before surgery."*

ANKLES ARTIFICIALLY CONSTRUCTED COMING NEXT

The latest that is now being introduced is a prosthetic device for the ankles. At a recent meeting of the American Academy of Orthopedic Surgeons, Dr. Richard Smith explained how this prosthetic device has been developed. He pointed out that of the first eleven cases on whom these devices have been tried, two failed to obtain relief and "since had their ankle bones fused."** Here again the claim is not one of correction but of relief. These operations do not rebuild the patient's broken joints, and in no way stop the joints from deteriorating further.

Concluding the discussion about these artificially constructed joints, we cannot help thinking of the ninety-one-year-old man who refused to submit to a hip-replacement

---

*"First Shoulder Prosthesis Are Implanted"—Medical News, *Journal of the American Medical Association*, March 25, 1974.
**"*Journal of the American Medical Association*, Medical News, April 1, 1974, "Arthritic Patients Take First Step With Ankle Prosthesis."

operation because a famous arthritis specialist whom he consulted, warned him against it. He told him, "You hear of the fifty that are better, but don't hear of the fifty that are worse." And even when pain is relieved because the broken-down joints have been cut out, what about the arthritis in other joints, or the overall and long-term effect of these operations?

We do not question the skill and the ingenuity that has gone into the development of these prosthetic devices. They have their place, but why not provide arthritis sufferers with the right kind of care during the early stages of the disease and thereby prevent the deterioration from progressing to the point where these operations may have to be considered?

SOME OTHER TYPES OF SURGERY

While discussing hip, knee, shoulder, and ankle-replacement surgery, we should mention that other types of surgery have been offered through the years to sufferers from arthritis. In some cases surgery is suggested to scrape away the calcium deposits that accumulate in the diseased or damaged joint, but it is well known that this does not stop new calcium from depositing in the joints, and the long-term effect of this type of surgery is questionable.

SPINAL FUSION OFFERS NO SOLUTION

We also have seen a great many cases where surgery was employed to fuse the vertebrae of the lower part of the back to relieve acute disc problems. In many of these cases the pain after the operation is often as bad as before the surgery. Nothing has really been accomplished so far as rebuilding the health of the patient is concerned.

REMOVING PART OF A VERTEBRA NOT THE ANSWER

Some patients are subjected to an operation known as a laminectomy, a type of surgical procedure to cut away a posterior portion of a vertebra to relieve pressure on the painful and inflamed nerve. Alan T., a young attorney who suffered pains of a most excruciating nature in the lower part of his back, was finally told by a noted New York surgeon that the only way he could get relief would be to submit to a laminectomy and a spinal fusion.

Then a neurosurgeon and a bone specialist warned him that no one can vouch for the outcome of these operations. So Alan said to himself, "What assurance have I that after the operation I'll feel any better?" This finally made him adopt the kind of care that we outlined for him and he has never needed the operation.

Only recently Dr. Henry W. Apfelbach of the orthopedic department, Abraham Lincoln School of Medicine of the University of Illinois, in a talk to surgeons at the American Academy of Orthopedic Surgeons in San Francisco, pointed to the poor results that often follow low back operations, and then stated that "repeated back surgery frequently gives rise to a greater state of ill-being." He suggested, instead, an injection into the damaged lumbar disc. If this fails, the patient can still have a laminectomy.

Dr. Brian H. Huncke, Clinical Assistant Professor of Orthopedic Surgery at Rush Medical College, confirmed Dr. Apfelbach's view on the subject.*

In discussing the different types of surgery that are being offered to the sufferer of arthritis, we wish to emphasize that we do not in any way minimize the skill or the ability of the surgeon, nor do we fail to recognize that these operations at times serve a useful purpose—especially when this is all that can be done to restore a patient to a more normal way of living.

*"Disc Injections Help Some Failed Laminectomy Cases." *Journal of the American Medical Association*, July 14, 1975.

CHAPTER 20

ARE THE DAYS OF MIRACLES PAST?

If anybody tells you that the days of miracles are past, don't believe it! Miracles happen every moment of the day. The seed that starts sprouting and then evolves into a full grown plant, the flower that blooms, the tree that bears fruit and provides the seeds from which other trees grow, the child born, who with time grows into full manhood or womanhood, are all miracles. And when we learn how to reawaken the healing powers of the body to rebuild the health of a desperately ailing and apparently hopelessly ill person, this too is one of nature's great miracles. A case now under our care illustrates this most vividly.

MRS. S.'s STORY

Because of an extremely heavy work schedule we have had to give up making house calls. About a year ago, however, a patient whose mother was desperately ill, and who, as she said, was failing rapidly, pleaded with us to visit her mother and see what we could do to help her. And to make sure that we would not refuse, she promised to drive us to her mother's home every time we were needed and return us to our office.

BODY RIDDLED WITH ARTHRITIS
When we examined the patient, we realized she was a seriously ill person in her seventies, suffering from a severe

form of arthritis. Virtually every one of her joints was riddled with the disease. Her legs and feet were badly swollen and thickened, while the degenerative changes in many of her joints had already progressed to the point where nobody could be certain whether anything could still be done to bring about a certain degree of improvement. Her knees were so greatly enlarged that they appeared to be about three times normal size. Her back, her neck, her shoulders, and many of her other joints showed advanced signs of breakdown. Every time her body was moved she was in agony, while turning from one side to the other was sheer torture. This made the life of her seventy-nine-year-old husband most difficult because when he had to get up many times during the night to help her find a more comfortable position, he was deprived of his sleep.

HEART AND CIRCULATION BADLY DAMAGED

While her broken down and badly crippled joints had already reached a greatly advanced stage, other even more serious health problems complicated the picture. There was a history of what her previous doctor indicated was a significant attack of congestive heart failure which had left her with a badly damaged heart and severely impaired blood vessels. Looking at her legs and feet, all you could see besides the heavy crippling and swelling, were the heavy markings and discoloration that show up in cases of phlebitis of long standing.

For years this patient had been kept on pain-killing drugs. Later came sleeping pills. Then, because of her badly damaged heart and broken-down circulatory system, she was put on digitalis, and more recently diuretics. Her weight at one time had been about 210 pounds, but with the water pills it came down to 192 pounds. This was her weight when we first saw her. All that the doctor who had taken care of her in the past could offer was medication that provided some measure of relief. He insisted that she would have to continue taking the water pills and the digitalis for the rest of her life; the pain-killing drugs already had become routine.

Such was the picture when we first visited this lady about a year ago. Her body was so badly deteriorated that we couldn't help wondering whether it would be advisable for us to become involved in the case. But we must never forget what even the most broken-down body can often accomplish when it is provided with the right kind of care. So we decided to try and see what our care could accomplish for her.

PAIN-KILLING PILLS, SLEEPING PILLS, AND WATER PILLS DISCONTINUED

Here in essence is an outline of the plan on which this patient was started: Our first instructions were that all pain-killing and sleeping pills be discontinued. When you deal with a patient whose body has become dependent on these drugs, this is not always easy and sometimes has to be done gradually. Then, since water pills can be highly damaging to the kidneys and to the overall body chemistry, they too were discontinued even though at first we were not sure but that she would have to return to them again, at least on a temporary basis.

TAMPERING WITH DIGITALIS RISKY BUSINESS

When it came to digitalis, however, the medication that is often prescribed to provide relief for a broken-down and weakened heart, the situation was entirely different. She had been kept on one digitalis pill daily, and because of her past history and the greatly worn-out and weakened condition of her heart, we felt that it would be inadvisable to take her off this medication at least at the start. About a week or two later, however, she was instructed to take her daily digitalis pill for six days and omit it on the seventh day. Later she was told to take it for five days and omit it on the sixth day. Still later she was to take it for four days and skip it on the fifth day. Then, she was to take it for three days and go without it every fourth day. This is the present dosage.

FOOD HABITS WERE CHANGED

Next to eliminating the pain-killing medicines and the water pills and reducing the intake of digitalis, she was placed on a carefully regulated dietary regimen. At first, she was kept only on fresh fruit until evening, taking only one kind of fruit at a time whenever hungry, or about every two or three hours. Then for the evening meal, a finely grated raw vegetable salad with a baked potato (without salt or butter), or a small portion of lean fish or chicken, and one steamed vegetable if still hungry, were permitted.

Later, her diet was modified to the point where for breakfast she could have any fresh fruit she wanted, for lunch, a raw vegetable salad and a baked potato with no butter or salt, and for dinner, a raw vegetable salad, a small portion of lean fish or chicken, or one lamb chop, and one steamed vegetable.

Two days a week she was to be kept on fresh fruit only, all day until evening, and then for the evening meal, the noon or evening menu described above.

MILD PHYSICAL EXERCISES STARTED

Then she was instructed to start with deep breathing and other mild physical exercises. She was to exercise regularly every morning and evening, and as she became stronger other more vigorous exercises were gradually added.

DAILY MUSTARD FOOT BATHS

Whenever possible, we insist that these patients take a comfortable hot epsom salt bath daily, either before retiring or at any other convenient time of the day, but because of this patient's badly crippled condition, getting in or out of a bathtub was out of the question. To make up for this, a hot mustard foot bath was suggested once or twice daily.

RESULTS TO DATE

Now after about one year of this type of care, what has been accomplished? Her badly swollen and deformed knees have returned to almost normal size. The pains in some of her joints have diminished considerably, in others they have disappeared almost entirely. Turning from one side to the other is no longer a problem. She can do it now with hardly any help and most often even without help. She is now able to walk from one room to the other, and to the porch, although slowly. She still has to use a walker to do it. She has also been taken out a number of times for rides in the car, something that nobody ever dreamt would be possible. She is not as yet ready to run and dance, but she is finally beginning to realize that she is on the road to better health.

SENSIBLE WEIGHT REDUCTION HELPFUL

This patient is now down to 155 pounds and anybody who understands the hazards of excess weight should realize what this means and how dangerous too much weight can be to a broken-down heart and to crippled joints.

REDUCING DIGITALIS A PROBLEM

So far, so good, but there remained one problem that troubled us, her dependence on digitalis. We had good reason to want to get her off this medication. Doctors know that digitalis is toxic and could be implicated in the deaths of some who take it. Some of our most noted cardiologists, Paul Dudley White, Arthur M. Master, and others, tell us how toxic this drug is. Only recently Dr. D. J. Chodos reminded us that in an editorial in the *Journal of the American Medical Association* (229, 1918, 1974), Dr. Aaguard had warned its readers that "it [digitalis] is a frequent cause of serious drug reactions." He then referred to Burch who in a recent article in *Postgraduate Medicine* (55–165, 1974) suggested that "digitalis toxicity could be implicated in the death of 0.2% to 2% (possibly up to 8%) of all patients receiving digitalis"*

On the other hand, reducing the medication too rapidly or omitting it entirely when the heart is no longer able to do its work adequately without it, can be risky. We also felt that whatever is to be done about it from here on, should be supervised by the medical doctor who originally prescribed it

Journal of the American Medical Association, March 31, 1975.

for her, since he lived closer to her home, could watch her, and when necessary make the needed adjustments.

THE FAMILY DOCTOR STEPS IN

However, when the doctor who had taken care of our patient learned about the type of care she was now receiving. he refused at first to have anything to do with the case. Later, however, after our patient's husband had a heart-to-heart talk with him, he relented and asked that she be brought to the hospital where he would subject her to a most thorough checkup.

WHAT DID HE FIND?

He was amazed when he noted how greatly she had improved. He was delighted with her loss of weight. He found that her heart had become much strengthened and this also pleased him. He found her circulation and her joints were in much healthier condition. "It's just a miracle!," was all that he could say. Then turning to an associate who was with him in the examining room at that time and who was also acquainted with the case, he said, "The results are most astonishing, I cannot believe it. It is actually a miracle."

SOLVING THE DIGITALIS PROBLEM

Of course this did not solve the problem of her digitalis, so we decided to call the doctor to see whether we could not get him to do something about it. As soon as we mentioned our name, you should have heard what he said! "It's fantastic what you have accomplished! I never thought that this could be done." After telling him how much we appreciated his cooperation, we brought up the question of digitalis, but he felt that, considering her past history, he would not like to do anything about it, at least for the time being. He promised, however, to keep on observing her to see whether eventually the medication couldn't be reduced even further.

ONLY A START

We are not fooling ourselves. We know that we cannot give our patient a new heart. But the care that she had so far received has done much to strengthen her heart, and we hope that with time it will continue to get even stronger. As far as her arthritis is concerned, the results are actually phenomenal. During all these months she has been without a single painkiller, her badly swollen and crippled knees and other broken-down joints have considerably improved, and we are hopeful that with time a great deal more will be accomplished. This in itself is a miracle.

Since this writing some months ago, still greater progress is reported. The lady is now able to visit her beautician regularly; she is being brought by car to our office for her treatments, and on this last Thanksgiving Day, visited her son in a neighboring town where, she said, "We had a sumptuous meal."

LANIE'S EXPERIENCE WITH OUR CARE

Another arthritis sufferer who tells us what the miraculous healing powers of her body have done to bring about her recovery, is Lanie J. Describing how sick she was, Lanie writes:

"I arrived in your office in a taxi, as I was afraid to strain my knees which at that time were swelling—rising and ebbing like an irregular tide—I never knew when I'd have to take a taxi to work or how long I'd have to be limping around or if I should call the MD who had diagnosed the problem as rheumatoid arthritis to see if he would advise more aspirin or else draining my knee (or knees, sometimes) surgically."

Lanie then continues: "Since that first visit to you, I have arrived in a taxi only one other time—when my body had a crisis reaction you had predicted and prepared me for. My left knee got very swollen then, but you saw me through—and without any drugs or surgery at all. It returned to normal size and since then, about six months ago, there has been no swelling in either knee and for about the last month I have been able to run and jump again, after having had arthritis for about two years and not being sure I would ever be able to move freely!"

Lanie then continues: "Due to your program and the many treatments you gave me at your office (and probably the 20-minute walks between your office and the train station, except for the two taxi rides), I am feeling better than I ever have before. What arthritis symptoms I have are a bare minimum and seem to occur at wider and wider intervals. I never have headaches, colds or menstrual cramps anymore. I look so well that my friends both with and without health problems are asking how does one get to see you. I feel more relaxed than I ever have and through my experience with you I believe I have gained a faith in life and the ways of nature I would never have thought possible."

She then concludes: "If there's such a thing as a natural miracle then I believe in miracles!—because your way of treatment which is so beautifully simple is like a miracle in this overly technologized time of fragmented understanding and treatment of the many parts of a person separately without ever seeing the whole. All one has to do is patiently follow your program, and just like a seed getting ready to germinate one day you'll start noticing this pain is gone, this swelling has gone down—and you'll keep feeling better gradually and one day be able to look back and realize you're an entirely new person and also look ahead and expect to feel even better."

CONNIE B.'S CASE

Connie B. was another very difficult arthritis patient who can tell how, by persisting with the care that we outlined for her, she finally regained her health.

When fifty-four-year-old Connie B. came to us in search of help, her knees had already broken down to the point where all that the doctor could suggest was an operation that would remove her own knee joints and replace them with joints built out of steel and plastic.

But then, after about three months of our type of care, Connie was rid of practically all her arthritis pains, and now about one year later, she is so well that she is able to lead a practically normal life. And when you talk to her about her recovery, all she keeps saying is "Just think what would have happened to me if I hadn't come to you for help."

When Connie started with our type of care, she too was greatly overweight. At that time she weighed 196 pounds, but then with time her weight ultimately came down to 167. Recently, however, since she has been feeling so well, she is not as careful as she should be, and as a result is putting on weight again. She is now back to 177 pounds. This is a pity since, as we keep telling her, to keep well, the healthful way of living has to become a lifetime habit. Otherwise the body will only break down again. Her weight gain shows the direction in which she is heading.

CHAPTER 21

YOUR CHANCE—DON'T THROW IT AWAY!

Most of us are impatient, and arthritis sufferers are not an exception; they keep looking for a magic pill to restore their health. They seem to forget, or don't want to remember, that what they suffer today is the result of a lifetime of abuse or carelessness.

It is necessary to understand that before the health of the joints can be rebuilt, all the organs and systems of the body need to function normally. To achieve this requires intelligence, perseverance, and dedication. The type of care that has to be adopted must become a new way of life, with no backsliding, or mistakes that brought on the illness will bring about its return.

The body is made up of many joints, and when arthritis has reached an advanced stage, some of these joints may have become so badly deformed or twisted that even the best of care cannot restore them to normal shape or form. But good care will prevent further deterioration and more severe deformities. The bumps or enlargements often noted on finger joints are known as Heberdon's nodes; these seldom disappear entirely, but proper care often reduces their size considerably.

It takes time for the body to reorganize its defenses, to build up its reserves, and to overcome the damaging effects of years of wrong medication, and to bring about the changes that help to undo the existing damage. We have seen cases where recovery took place within a relatively short period of time, sometimes not more than a few months, but most of those who find their way to our care, come to it after years of suffering, and after the disease has made deep inroads. In these cases time and patience are required, and it is the height of folly to assume that the arthritis and its related ills can be uprooted so rapidly. It is necessary for the patient often to pass through a series of intermediate, sometimes acute, reactions before the disease is overcome. These reactions need not be frightening because they are not life-threatening.

MILDRED M.'s CASE

We mention this because of our experience with 57-year-old Mildred M. The first time we heard from Mildred was when she informed us that one of her friends, whose case history appears in an earlier chapter, urged her to consult us about her own arthritis problem.

In a letter, Mildred explained that she had started gold injections six years before the present time; that she had been kept on cortisone, prednisone, and various other anti-arthritic medicines, and that she was still on some of these medications. She also had consulted orthopedic surgeons who had recommended surgery for her hips and knees. She complained that her condition had deteriorated to the point where walking was extremely difficult and her entire body was full of aches and pains.

Mildred placed herself under our care, and what we found was just as she had described it. It took several months of intensive care and re-education before this patient succeeded in giving up cortisone; as she states in a letter to the friend who had referred her to us, "for Doctor Warmbrand, getting me off cortisone was a miracle."

DIFFICULTIES RESULTING FROM DRUG ADDICTION

We have stated that patients who have been kept on prednisone, cortisone, gold injections, butazolidin, indocin, or other pain-suppressive drugs for a long period of time, may have become so dependent on these remedies that their sudden withdrawal or discontinuance, is practically impossible and sometimes inadvisable. In these cases the drugs may have to be discontinued gradually, or agonizing withdrawal symptoms may make the life of the sufferer unbearable.

Even though it took several months for Mildred to stop taking cortisone, she nevertheless began to show a great deal of improvement and we hoped that ultimately she would be another one of our success stories. But about that time, Mildred decided to explore other possibilities, and she and her husband made the decision to give up their home and move to the West Coast. What happened after that was cataclysmic. We learned from a friend that Mildred regretted the move—she needed help and did not know to whom she could turn. Finally, she landed in a wheelchair.

What was worse, she drifted back to some of her previous unhealthful eating and living habits, and also to some of the pain-relieving remedies that she had depended on in the past. At last, in desperation, she decided to resort to surgery.

WHERE DID MILDRED GO WRONG?

It took years of illness and pain-killing medication before Mildred finally found her way to our type of care, and since it took months before we succeeded in getting her off cortisone, why didn't she have the patience to continue on her health-rebuilding program? We feel confident that had she continued with the care we had outlined for her, she would have continued to improve, and in time her joints could have been rebuilt to the point where surgery would not have been necessary. But as Mildred admits in a letter to a friend, she is both a strong and a weak creature. "I am afraid, and away from proper influences . . . were I on Dr.

Warmbrand's diet, I do know that I would have few, if any . . . complaints to tell about.''

To us she writes, "As time goes on I am more and more convinced that your way of life is the only, only way . . ." but she repeats that she needs somebody who can keep encouraging her, and how well it would be if Dr. Warmbrand would be her "Guru." Mildred's future is unpredictable, but there is still hope for her. We must point out that even those who are not too close to us can get well if they adopt our type of care and follow it faithfully. For inspiration and guidance they should turn to our books, and whenever possible place themselves under the care of a doctor or practitioner who takes care of his patients in accordance with our principles.

The moral of Mildred's story is, don't look for short cuts because they don't exist. Rebuilding the body is a day-by-day undertaking, and if you drift back to careless or haphazard ways of living, you will only pay for it with your health.

THE LESSON WE LEARNED FROM MRS. G.

It seems to us that this book would not be complete without the story of sixty-some-year-old Stella G. When several years ago Stella G. came for help, her spine was so badly deformed and damaged that nobody ever thought that she could be helped. She was all humped up, and she told us that in recent years she had shrunk to about half her size. We ordered X-rays, and here in essence is the report that we received from the laboratory:

"There are multiple compression fractures throughout the thoracic and lumbar spine, *the most marked in the lower thoracic region where there has been 50 to 60 per cent loss of height. There are associated degenerative changes throughout the spine.*" (emphasis ours)

The report further stated that "there has been some demineralization (osteoporosis) of the bones of the spine," and it then concluded with the summary:

"Multiple compression fractures as noted. There has been demineralization of the bones included in the study."

The X-rays further revealed multiple calcifications in the spleen, a reminder that when joints calcify or become arthritic, other organs or parts of the body are similarly affected in one way or another. This is why we are never surprised when we find that sufferers from arthritis often suffer from gallstones, kidney stones, hardening of the arteries, or some other ills where the tissues or organs have become hardened, thickened, or calcified.

This woman's spine was so badly deformed that we did not believe it could ever straighten out or that Mrs. G. could ever regain her normal figure. All that we thought was that we would be able to provide her with a certain amount of relief and possibly bring about sufficient improvement to make her life more bearable.

CHANGES ONE YEAR LATER

But you should see what a year of care—based upon conscientious adherence to the instructions that she received with regard to diet, baths, a well-planned program of physical exercises, plenty of rest and sleep, has done for her. Her hump has practically disappeared. She has grown taller and more slender, actually taller by many inches. And she no longer suffers any of the pains or discomforts that made her life so miserable in the past.

About a year after her recovery we asked Mrs. G. to have her spine X-rayed again. We wanted visual proof of what had been accomplished. She no longer felt that this was necessary and in a way she was right. Her appearance, the way she walked, and what she is now able to do, give living proof of the remarkable transformation that has taken place in her case.

THE LATEST ON MRS. G.

The last time we saw Mrs. G. was only a few weeks before we turned this manuscript over to the publisher. She was working in the garden and around the house, and when she straightened out she looked tall, trim and fit—years younger than when she first came to see us. When we told her how well she looked, her reply was, "Why shouldn't I? You helped me when everybody thought that there was no longer any hope for me. I'll never forget that. I keep up with my diet and the exercises, and hope to stay well for life."

TURN TO NATURE'S TREASURES

There is a saying among the young: "Gather ye rosebuds while ye may." The arthritis sufferer must do something similar. The treasures that nature has so lavishly and freely bestowed upon us are everywhere, and all of us can use them freely. Use them consistently and faithfully, never deviate from your course, and the benefits that you will derive will be infinite.

BECOME A MESSENGER OF HEALTH

In our many years of practice we have seen countless seemingly hopeless arthritic patients who, by adhering to the program that we present in this book, succeeded not only in regaining their health, but in becoming messengers of health. They are living examples of what this type of care can do for those who are suffering from a highly debilitating and often crippling disease, and they serve as an inspiration to others who are in need of help. You, too, can become one of them. Start now, follow the right path consistently and faithfully, and a new and healthful life will open up for you.

APPENDIX

RECIPES FOR ARTHRITIS PATIENTS

When we talk of the kind of food that the arthritis sufferer needs if he is to get well, we do not mean that he has to deprive himself of enjoyable food. What he must do is change from food that fails to provide his body with necessary nourishment to food that helps to rebuild it.

In these pages we present a variety of dishes that are not only wholesome but also most enjoyable. But always keep in mind the need for periodic fasting periods, the importance of not overeating, and of eating only when really hungry. Whenever possible, include an abundance of fresh fruits and uncooked vegetables in your dietary plan.

To show you how good the meals of the arthritis patient can be, even when at first the choice may seem somewhat limited, we offer this appendix with some of the dishes that our patients have relished most.

We shall start with a series of recipes for raw vegetable and fresh fruit salads. Raw vegetables and fruits are not only enjoyable and tasty, but they provide easily digestible carbohydrates, the finest protein, and contain vitamins, minerals, enzymes, co-enzymes, trace elements—all the essential food elements needed to rebuild the health of the body.

Those who suffer not only from arthritis, but from accompanying digestive disorders may have to exclude raw vegetables and fresh fruits from their diets at first, and we have included some recipes to satisfy this problem. But patients with digestive disorders should adopt a plan of living to correct this condition, allowing them to add essential raw foods gradually to their diets.

BODY AND HEALTH-BUILDING RAW VEGETABLE AND FRUIT SALADS

RAINBOW SALAD

1 carrot, 1 beet, 1/2 cucumber or zucchini, 1 stalk of celery, 1/2 parsnip, small portion of turnip, a small portion of cabbage (red or green or both), several leaves of romaine lettuce or any other greens, small amount of parsley or watercress, a small onion or a few scallions, a portion of ripe avocado, some sprouts (mung or alfalfa sprouts, if available). Add lemon to flavor.

Whenever possible use organically grown vegetables; otherwise peel—some of them may be heavily waxed. Grate carrot, beet, parsnip, cabbage and cucumber or zucchini. Cut up the celery; dice the onion or scallions, and serve on lettuce leaves. Add parsley or watercress and sprouts. Add mashed avocado, and flavor with lemon juice. Serve with baked potatoes, natural brown rice, yams or small portions of any of the lean protein dishes. One or two steamed vegetables may be added to the meal if desired. This makes a satisfying meal.

OTHER ENJOYABLE RAW VEGETABLE SALADS

CHLOROPHYL SALAD

Take a cucumber, several varieties of lettuce, such as romaine, escarole, chickory and others, several sprigs of watercress, 3 stalks of celery, amount of sprouts desired and 1 or 2 scallions.

Chop all the vegetables including the lettuce; add a portion of avocado and serve with lemon juice, honey dressing or any other favorite dressing. If dressing is made with oil, use olive oil or polyunsaturated vegetable oils.

SUNSET SALAD

1/2 head of green cabbage, 1/2 lb. crisp raw spinach, 2 carrots, one bunch of red radishes, 1/2 cucumber, small onion (chop, do not grate).

Make bed of spinach. Shred cabbage, grate carrots and turnip. Place in separate mounds on spinach. Thinly slice onion and put in center of dish. Surround by red radishes. Serve with lemon, oil and honey or other favorite dressing. Serves four.

GREEN SALAD

1 cup chopped dandelion leaves, 1 cup chopped chickory or Chinese cabbage, 1/2 head chopped lettuce, 1/2 cup chopped fresh spinach, 1/2 cup chopped watercress, 1/4 cup finely chopped parsley, 2 stalks of celery.

Mix all vegetables together and serve with lemon juice and honey. Add a sprinkling of grated or chopped nuts or sunflower or pumpkin or sesame seeds or 1 tablespoon of nut butter. Serves four.

APPLE AND VEGETABLE SALAD

2 apples, 4 scallions, 2 stalks of celery, 6 to 8 romaine lettuce leaves.
Chop vegetables, shred apples and mix. Add chopped or finely grated unroasted sunflower or pumpkin seeds or almonds and serve with your favorite dressing.

BAKED EGGPLANT SALAD

1 good sized eggplant, 2 stalks green celery, 2 large or 3 small carrots, 2 medium onions.

Bake eggplant in skin, peel and mash in wooden bowl with a wooden spoon. Chop celery, carrots and onion, add to eggplant, and mix thoroughly. Serve on lettuce leaves. For dressing add lemon or lime juice and vegetable oil. Serve with baked potatoes.

SALAD SUPREME

3 carrots, medium size; 2 beets, medium size; 1/4 head cabbage, medium size; 1/4 lb. spinach, 1 large onion, 1 green pepper, 2 tomatoes, 8 radishes, 1 small avocado.

Dice onions in separate dish. Add olive oil or any other vegetable oil. Cover dish tightly and let stand in refrigerator for 1 to 2 hours. Grate carrots, beets and cabbage; cut spinach fine and place each vegetable in separate mounds.

Add the diced onion to each vegetable mound. Cut green peppers into strips, slice tomatoes and use whole radishes for garnishing. Add slices of avocado. Use lemon juice or lime juice and honey dressing, if desired. Serves three.

TASTY SALAD

1 cup shredded cabbage, 1 grated carrot, 6 ripe olives, 1 clove of garlic, 1/2 cup diced green pepper, 1/2 cup diced celery.

Rub a clove of garlic on salad bowl and toss in all the vegetables. Cut in olives and mix well. Add your favorite dressing. Serves two.

DELICIOUS COLE SLAW

1 small head green cabbage, 3 stalks celery, 2 large carrots, 3/4 cup finely-cut parsley, 1 large green or red sweet pepper.

Wash and grate vegetables. Make dressing of 2 tbs. oil and juice of 1 lemon. Pour over vegetables and mix thoroughly.

BRIGHT RED SALAD

1/4 head red cabbage, 2 small onions, 2 medium carrots, 1/4 cup raisins, 1 beet.

Shred cabbage, carrots and beet. Mix with raisins. Add sliced onions and serve with lemon or fresh lime juice and vegetable oil or yogurt dressing. Serves two.

CABBAGE DELIGHT

1/2 small green cabbage, 1 stalk celery, 2 sweet apples, 1/4 lb. shelled nuts.

Chop together and serve with a border of watercress, escarole or chicory. Flavor with lemon juice, if desired, before serving, or any other favorite dressing. Serves two.

CABBAGE-APPLE SALAD

1 cup shredded cabbage, 1 1/2 shredded apples, 1 stalk celery, 1 beet, 1 carrot, 1 tbs. raisins.

Mince celery, grate carrot and beet, add shredded cabbage, apples and raisins, and mix well. Serve with lemon and honey, eggless mayonnaise or your favorite dressing. Serves two.

CARROT-RAISIN SURPRISE

4 carrots, 4 sweet apples, 2 stalks celery, 1 cup seedless raisins, 1/2 cup chopped or grated nuts.

Shred carrots and apples. Cut or dice celery fine. Add raisins and mix. Sprinkle chopped or grated nuts and serve on lettuce leaves. Serves four.

GREEN SALAD #1

1 cup fresh green peas, 2 stalks green celery, 1 medium or two small onions or some fresh scallions, 1 green pepper, 2 small ripe tomatoes, small amount of grated cauliflower.

Dice stalk and heart of celery, onions or scallions, pepper and tomatoes. Grate cauliflower. Mix together and add green peas. Serve on lettuce leaves. Your favorite nut butter dissolved with lemon juice makes a fine dressing. Serves two.

GREEN SALAD #2

1 cup fresh green peas, 1/2 head small green cabbage, 1/2 head small green lettuce, 2 leaves spinach.

Chop cabbage with small quantity of chives or leek. Shred lettuce and spinach. Add green peas and serve with fresh lime or lemon juice or eggless mayonnaise. Serves two.

POTATO SALAD DELIGHT

1 large potato, 2 small onions, 1 stalk green celery, 1 green pepper, 1 carrot, 1 ripe avocado, small amount of watercress.

Steam potato in jacket. Peel and dice while still hot. Chop onions, celery, carrot and pepper. Mix and serve on lettuce leaves and watercress. Add ripe mashed avocado and minced parsley. Serve with desired dressing.

HEALTH POTATO SALAD

2 lbs. boiled potatoes, 1 large green pepper, 3 stalks celery, 3/4 cups finely cut parsley, 1 large onion, 1 avocado.

Peel potatoes and cut into cubes. Grate vegetables. Mix vegetables with potatoes. Add diced avocado. Make a dressing of 1 tablespoon oil and juice of one lemon. Mix dressing thoroughly and pour over potato salad. Mix again and let stand in refrigerator for at least one hour before serving. Serves four.

VEGETABLE PROTEIN SALAD

3 cups finely shredded cabbage, 1 cup shredded carrots, 2 medium tomatoes, 1 diced green pepper, 1 lb. cottage, or pot cheese. Serve on lettuce leaves.

TOSSED SALAD

4 tbs. grated carrot, 3 tbs. diced celery, 2 tbs. diced onion, 4 tbs. chopped red cabbage, 8 red radishes, 8 ripe olives, 1 ripe tomato, 1 avocado, peeled and sliced lengthwise, chopped parsley (to flavor).

Mix carrots, celery, onion, cabbage, radishes, olives and parsley together and place in the center of plate. Surround with ring of tomato slices and arrange avocado pieces over top of mixture. Squeeze lemon juice over avocado. Serves two.

PEPPER SURPRISE

4 green or red sweet peppers, 1/2 lb. cottage or pot cheese, 1/2 cup seedless raisins, 2 large grated apples.

Mix cheese, raisins and apples. Stuff peppers. Fine with relish "Deluxe" or any other favorite relish or dressing. Serves four.

STUFFED TOMATO SALAD

1 cup cottage or pot cheese, 1 small onion, 1 cup raw spinach, 1 stalk celery, 4 tomatoes.

Chop onion, spinach and celery. Scoop out tomatoes and mix with cheese. Add chopped vegetables and mix all together with eggless mayonnaise. Stuff tomatoes and serve on lettuce leaves. Garnish with parsley or watercress. Serves two. Makes an ideal lunch.

VEGETABLE FRUIT DELIGHT #1

1 cup of cottage or pot cheese or fresh shredded coconut, 1/2 lb. raisins, 1/2 lb. fresh peaches, 1/2 lb. apricots, 1/2 lb. fresh cherries.

Cut fruit into small parts, remove pits. Add raisins. Mix with cheese or coconut and serve on green lettuce leaves. Fresh fruit juices make a fine dressing. Serves two.

VEGETABLE FRUIT DELIGHT #2

1 quart blueberries (in season), 1/2 pineapple, 4 carrots, 1 ripe banana, 1 lb. cottage cheese.

Shred carrots. Cube pineapple. Mix well together with cheese, add sliced banana and berries and serve on bed of green lettuce leaves. Serves four.

WALDORF SALAD #1

1 cup diced unsulphured apricots, 1 cup diced sweet apple, 1/2 cup diced green celery, 1 tablespoon chopped nuts or nut butter or nut meal.

Mix and serve, using favorite dressing. Serves two.

WALDORF SALAD #2

1/2 cup shredded green cabbage, 1/2 cup shredded green celery, 1 cup finely shredded apple, 1/2 cup seedless raisins, 1/4 cup shredded nut or nut meal.

Mix and serve on green lettuce leaves. If dressing is desired, use one-half ripe mashed avocado. Add lemon juice or eggless mayonnaise if desired. Serves two.

COLORFUL FRUIT SALAD #1

2 tbs. raspberries, 2 tbs. blueberries, 3 tbs. honeydew melon balls, 3 tbls. canteloupe balls, 1 ripe banana.

Place fruit on crisp lettuce leaves, place slices of banana around it. Serve with pineapple juice and honey. Serves one.

COLORFUL FRUIT SALAD #2

1 pear, 1 peach, 1 apple, 1/2 cup grapes, 1 tbs. raisins, 1 ripe banana.

Slice the fruits, halve the grapes, add raisins and mix. Serve on lettuce leaves with a nut butter dressing and honey. Serves one.

MARINATED SALAD

1 small green cabbage (shredded), 2 cups shredded or grated carrots, 1 green pepper (diced), 1 cucumber (diced).

Prepare dressing, one cup equal portions of lemon juice, oil and honey, and pour over salad. Cover and place in refrigerator for one hour before serving. Serve on green lettuce leaves. Serves two or three.

ZESTFUL DRESSINGS, RELISHES AND SAUCES

Vegetables and fruits have their own delicate and often exotic flavors, but those who have become accustomed to sharp irritating spices and condiments may have already dulled their taste buds so that at first they have to reach for some special dressings, relishes and sauces to enhance the flavor of their food. For them the following salad dressings, relishes and sauces add valuable nutrients to meals.

AVOCADO DRESSINGS

#1 Ripe Avocado mashed, with the addition of lemon juice.

#2 Ripe Avocado mashed, with minced onions and lemon juice, to taste.

#3 Ripe Avocado mashed and mixed with tomato juice, garlic powder and lemon juice, to taste. (Mashed ripe avocado keeps better if the pit, or seed, is retained and added.)

FRENCH DRESSING

3/4 cup tomato juice, 1 or 2 tbs. soy oil, juice of 1/3 lemon, half clove garlic or a little grated onion. Shake well before serving.

OIL AND LEMON DRESSING #1
Soy oil and lemon juice, well blended, or whipped with a fork.

OIL AND LEMON DRESSING #2
Olive oil, lemon juice, equal parts, and garlic to taste, if desired.

SPECIAL FRENCH DRESSING
Olive oil, lemon juice and honey—equal parts.

NUT-PINEAPPLE DRESSING
Grind nuts and raisins. Add pineapple juice and few drops of lemon. Save the liquid from drained sliced fresh pineapple, or crush pineapple and squeeze juice out. Add a little honey.

NUT BUTTER DRESSING
Almond, pecan or coconut butter. Dilute one part of nut butter to six parts of water and add lemon juice to taste. Nut butters are obtainable in health food stores.

DELIGHTFUL YOGURT DRESSING
1 cup yogurt with 2 tbs. honey. Whip together. Makes a delicious dressing over fresh and stewed fruits, berries and puddings. Sprinkle a little wheat germ, if desired.

CAULIFLOWER RELISH
1 1/2 cups grated raw cauliflower, 1/2 cup minced scallions, 1 diced tomato, 1/2 cup raw grated carrot.

Mix with lemon juice and honey or eggless mayonnaise to taste.

LEMON OR LIME HONEY DRESSING
1/3 cup of lemon or lime juice, 1/3 cup vegetable oil, 1/2 cup honey, 1 tsp. celery or poppy seeds.

Combine all ingredients. Beat with rotary beater until blended and smooth. Serve over fruit salads.

RELISH "DE LUXE"
 1 cup diced cucumber, 1/2 cup diced ripe olives, 1/2 cup minced green pepper, 1/2 cup diced red radishes, 1/2 cup minced pimento, 1/4 cup minced parsley.

Mix with tomato juice dressing to which garlic and onion have been added.

EGGLESS MAYONNAISE
 Mash ripe banana. Add oil and lemon juice, drop by drop, and keep beating with fork until it reaches the right consistency.

FARM FOOD SPECIAL
 This dressing is being served at the Farmfood restaurant in New York at special dinners and banquets and has been acclaimed by all who have tried it.

Mix 2 tbs. yogurt, 2 tbs. honey, 3 tbs. salad oil, juice of 1/2 lemon, 2 cloves of garlic, mashed well. Serves four.

BEET RELISH (A Florida Spa Special)
 Slice or dice cooked beets. Slice or dice raw onions. In a quart jar, place a layer of beets, then a layer of onions, until jar is filled. Add the juice of two lemons and a few drops of honey. Then fill the jar with water and close tight. Let stand for several days.

SOME DELIGHTFUL BEVERAGES
We do not as a rule encourage beverages or liquids with meals; it is best that they be taken between meals. Fruit or vegetable juices are usually best, and when a hot beverage is desired the finely flavored herb teas, such as alfalfa tea, camomile tea, strawberry leaf, comfrey tea, lin-

denblossom tea, or sassafras tea gently sweetened with honey, or a cup of clear vegetable broth are good.

ALFALFA-SEED BEVERAGE ESPECIALLY VALUABLE

A beverage that is enjoyable and beneficial to arthritis sufferers is the alfalfa seed beverage. Add six teaspoonfuls of organically grown alfalfa seeds to one cup of water. Let stand overnight, then bring to a boil. Keep boiling for ten minutes, lower the flame and continue to boil slowly, for another 15 minutes. Strain, cool, and sweeten gently with honey.

Don't waste the seeds; add them to your raw vegetable salad, or use them with any of the other vegetable dishes.

Other enjoyable and nourishing beverages are clear vegetable broth and fruit juices.

DEHYDRATED VEGETABLE POWDERS

Vegetable broth powder, fine for soup stock, steamed and baked dishes, is made of dehydrated powdered vegetables, and is obtainable in health food stores. It may also be found in the food departments of some of the larger department stores. (Be sure to buy the unsalted brand.)

Garlic powder, onion powder, celery powder and tomato powder are also obtainable in health food stores and make flavorful additions to salads, soups and vegetable dishes, as do caraway seeds, paprika, marjoram, sage, savory, onions, tomatoes, garlic, green peppers, thyme, watercress, celery, pimento, parsley and dill.

NOURISHING SOUPS

Many feel that a meal without a soup is not complete. Yet the most essential part in a soup is its stock and not the water which has been added to it.

The soups that we list in this section are nourishing

and good but from a health point of view soup should not be included as a regular part of a meal more than once or twice a week. Cooked vegetable soups may be pureed in an electric blender.

BEET SOUP

2 bunches beets, 2 tbs. honey, 2 soft tomatoes, 1 onion, 5 glasses water, juice of 3/4 lemon.

Remove the leaves of beets. Scrub beets and stem; and slice or shred them. Add water, tomatoes and onion, and boil for 30 minutes or until beets are soft. Add lemon and honey and serve either hot or cold. Save the beet leaves for salad. When chilled, the addition of cucumber, cottage cheese, and yogurt makes this beet soup a treat. Serves six.

BEET SOUP FAVORITE

Liquefy cooked whole beets in a blender. Add lemon juice to taste and a little honey if desired. Serve hot or cold. Yogurt or clabbered milk may be added. Fine in combination with potatoes boiled in their jackets.

CORN CHOWDER

4 cobs of corn, 3 glasses of water, 4 carrots.

Cut kernels from cobs. Cut carrots into fine strips. Steam carrots 12 minutes. Add the corn. Steam 5 minutes more and serve. Serves four.

DRIED FRUIT SOUP

1/2 cup dried apricots, 1/2 cup dried peaches, 1/2 cup dried cherries, 1/2 cup dried figs, 1/2 cup raisins. (All fruits should be unsulphured.)

Fruit may be used whole or diced. Use one cup of water to each 1/2 cup of fruit. Bring to a boil and simmer for 20 minutes. Cool and serve. Add honey and lemon if desired. Serves five.

GARDEN VEGETABLE SOUP

1 cup diced potatoes, 1 cup diced carrots, 1/2 cup shredded onion, 1 stalk celery (diced), 1/2 lb. string-beans (diced), 2 tomatoes or tomato juice.

Add vegetable broth powder to cold water. Bring to a boil. Add vegetables and simmer, for 30 minutes. Serves five.

LENTIL VEGETABLE SOUP

2 cups lentils (soaked), 3 carrots, 1 parsnip, 1 green pepper, 1/2 head celery.

Dice carrots, parsnip, celery and pepper. Mix vegetables and lentils. Add 6 cups of water. Bring to a boil and simmer for 30 minutes. Serves six.

POTATO SOUP #1

6 small potatoes, 1 onion, 2 stalks celery, 1 carrot, 1/2 cup green peas.

Dice all vegetables. Add 3 cups of water. Bring to boil and simmer for 30 minutes. Serve with a sprinkling of parsley greens and vegetable broth powder. Serves two.

POTATO SOUP #2

6 small potatoes, 2 small carrots, parsley or dill to flavor.

Dice potatoes and carrots. Add 2 tbs. chopped parsley. Mix together and add 3 cups of water. Bring to a boil and simmer for thirty minutes. Serves two.

STEAMED, STEWED AND BAKED VEGETABLE DISHES

These are the dishes that those who suffer from digestive disorders and who cannot handle uncooked vegetables and fruits, may have to turn to at first. For more specific advice to those who are confronted by a digestive problem, we suggest that you turn to our *Encyclopedia of Natural Health.* These ills will also be covered in our forthcoming book, *The Natural Approach To Ulcers and Other Digestive Disorders.*

BAKED ARTICHOKE TREAT
2 large artichokes, 2 cloves garlic, 2 tbs. oil.

Wash artichokes thoroughly by pouring hot water through the leaves. Place in water to cover halfway and cook until tender, about 40 minutes. Artichokes may be cooked in a pressure cooker (1/2 cup water; 15 min. at 15 lbs. pressure). Cut in half and add garlic, grated fine, between leaves. Sprinkle with oil and place into oiled baking dish. Bake for 20 minutes. Save water for soup. Serves two.

BOILED ARTICHOKES
2 large artichokes, sauce (as described below).

Wash artichokes as above. Place in water to cover halfway. Cook until leaves can pull off easily by folding back. Pour off water.

Sauce: Mix 2 cloves of garlic, grated fine, and some lemon juice in a little water. Add potato starch and vegetable broth powder, which were first dissolved in cold water and mixed into a paste. Boil for 10 to 12 minutes or until tender. Test with a fork to find out whether they are done. Dip inner portion of leaves in sauce and eat soft part. Serves two.

STEAMED ARTICHOKES
2 large artichokes, 2 tbs. vegetable oil, 2 cloves garlic.

Wash artichokes thoroughly by pouring hot water through the leaves. Steam for 45 minutes. Mash garlic and mix with oil and a few drops of lemon juice and tomato juice. Cut artichokes in half, pour dressing between leaves and serve. Serves two.

ASPARAGUS COMBINATION

1/2 lb. asparagus, 1/2 lb. green peas, 1 stalk celery, 1/2 cup tomato juice, 1 clove of pressed or grated garlic.

Wash asparagus clean of all sand. Add green peas and celery with tomato juice and garlic. Steam or bake for 20 to 25 minutes. Serves two.

BROCCOLI IN CASSEROLE

2 carrots, 1 bunch broccoli, 1/3 glass water, 2 stalks celery, 1/2 lb. green peas.

Place broccoli in casserole, add sliced carrots and celery, add water and cover. Bake 1/2 hour in medium oven. Sprinkle with vegetable broth powder or serve with your favorite sauce. Serves six.

STUFFED CABBAGE

12 green cabbage leaves (any kind desired, Savoy variety preferred, if available), 1 large sweet potato, 2 carrots, 1/2 cup seedless raisins.

Soak cabbage leaves in hot water, until tender. Cut away thick ribs in cabbage leaves. Grind other ingredients together. Add vegetable powder and a sprinkling of oil. Roll into cabbage leaves, bake for 30 minutes and serve. Serves six.

STUFFED CABBAGE REVELATION

12 cabbage leaves (green), Savoy cabbage preferred, 1 cup brown rice, 1/2 cup seedless raisins, 2 carrots, 1/2 cup green peas, 1 1/2 cups tomato juice, 2 ripe tomatoes, 1 green pepper, 1 large onion, 2 cloves garlic, 2 tbs. honey.

Pour 6 cups of boiling water over brown rice and soak for 3–4 hours. Keep pot covered. Steam in some water over low flame until tender, then add honey. Soak cabbage leaves 15 minutes in boiling water to soften for rolling. Meanwhile chop fine or grind raisins, carrots and green peas together and mix with steamed rice. Roll mixture in cabbage leaves, closing ends by folding the leaves inside. Cut up green pepper, slice onion, cut up tomatoes, grate garlic and add tomato juice. Steam 5 minutes. Drop the stuffed cabbage rolls slowly, one at a time, into the mixture and continue to steam until tender, keeping pot covered. Serves six.

CARROT DE LUXE

1 bunch carrots, 1/2 lb. fresh lima beans, 1 tbs. grated onion, 1 tbs. chopped parsley, 2 stalks celery (diced).

Steam carrots for about 12 minutes. Add onion, celery, beans, parsley to 1 cup boiling water. Simmer in covered pot 10 minutes and pour over carrots. Serves three.

CARROT STEW

1 bunch carrots, 1/2 bunch parsley, 1 sweet potato, 1 large onion, 1 parsnip, 1/2 knob celery, 2 tbs. honey.

Dice all vegetables. Add 1/2 cup water and honey. Steam until tender. Serves four.

EGGPLANT CASSEROLE #1

1 eggplant, 1 onion, 3 stalks of celery, 1/2 green pepper, 1/2 glass tomato juice.

Bake whole eggplant first. Remove skin after baking and mash. Add grated or diced onion, green pepper, diced celery and tomato juice. Bake in covered pan for 25 minutes. Serves four.

EGGPLANT CASSEROLE #2

1 medium ripe eggplant, 1 large or 2 medium onions, 1 clove of garlic, 1 large red or green pepper, 1 large or 2 small tomatoes, 1/2 cup of tomato juice.

Mash garlic and dice onion and pepper. Simmer for a few minutes in 1/4 cup tomato juice until parboiled. Scrub skin of eggplant well and cut into pieces. Add to parboiled garlic, onion and pepper. Add balance of tomato juice and tomato. Cover and steam all together for 15 minutes. A little oil and lemon juice or vegetable broth powder may be added before serving, if desired. Serves four.

EGGPLANT STEAK

1 eggplant, 1/4 bunch parsley, 1 small bunch endives or several leaves of Chinese cabbage.

Cut eggplant into inch slices. Sprinkle with wheat germ. Add 4 teaspoons oil and slice of onion. Bake slowly until brown and tender. Serve with chopped endive or Chinese cabbage. Sprinkle parsley over it. Serves four.

STEAMED EGGPLANT

1 medium eggplant, 1 green pepper, 2 ripe tomatoes, 2 tbs. celery powder or other vegetable powder, 2 onions, 2 tbs. vegetable oil.

Steam eggplant in skin 10 minutes. Slice onions and place in oiled baking dish. Slice eggplant and place in layers on top of onions. Cut pepper in long strips and place on eggplant. Slice tomatoes; place on pepper.

Sprinkle with celery powder or any other vegetable powder and a little oil, and bake in oiled dish for 35 minutes in moderate oven. (Celery powder may be omitted, if not available). Serves four.

STEAMED KALE
1 lb. kale, 1 onion, 2 tomatoes.

Wash kale thoroughly to remove grit. Slice onion and tomatoes. Place in waterless cooker or steamer and steam until tender, or use ordinary utensils and simmer on a low flame for 10 minutes. Serve with seasoning if desired. Serves three.

OKRA STEW #1
1 lb. okra, 2 large onions, 1 clove garlic, 3 tomatoes, 1/2 cup chopped parsley.

Wash and cut okra in halves. Steam okra 15 minutes. Add garlic, diced onions and tomatoes. Steam together 15 minutes more. Serve with a sprinkle of oil and vegetable broth powder, if desired. Serves four.

OKRA STEW #2
1 lb. okra, 1 sweet potato, 1 stalk celery, 1 green pepper.

Slice potato and dice other vegetables. Stew until tender. Serve with brown rice (already cooked). Sprinkle vegetable broth powder when serving. Serves four.

PARSNIP STEW
1 lb. parsnips, 1 large Bermuda onion, 1/2 glass tomato juice, 2 carrots, 1 tbs. oil.

Dice parsnips and carrots and mince onions. Add oil and tomato juice. Steam or bake 30 minutes until tender. Serves three.

STEAMED PEAS
1 lb. green peas in pods, 1 small onion.

Steam peas in pods until almost done. Remove from pods and cook with sliced onion for 5 minutes more.

Sprinkle a little vegetable broth powder. Serve either hot or cold. Serves two.

STUFFED PEPPERS

3 onions, 1 parsnip, a little parsley, 3 carrots, 1/2 bunch celery, 4 large green peppers.

Cut peppers into half lengths. Remove seeds and fill with scraped chopped carrots, parsnip, celery, parsley and onion. Place into oiled baking dish, and dash a little oil on top of vegetables. Bake 30 minutes. Pour tomato juice or any sauce preferred over cooked vegetables. A cheese sprinkle or baked potato or soybeans recommended with this. Serves four.

STUFFED PEPPER PIQUANT

1/2 cup cooked brown rice, 3 stalks celery, 2 carrots, 1/4 lb. green peas, 1 tsp. vegetable flavoring, 1/3 cup water or vegetable broth, 1 grated onion, 4 peppers.

Wash peppers, cut tops off and remove seeds. Mix parboiled rice with finely cut onions, diced celery, diced carrots and green peas in water or vegetable broth. Stuff peppers. Place in uncovered pan with 1/2 cup water or broth and bake in a moderate oven for 20 minutes. Serves four.

POTATO CUTLET

8 large potatoes, 2 cloves garlic, 1 stalk celery, 1 cup vegetable oil.

Scrub and shred potatoes on coarse grater. Grate or press garlic. Dice celery very fine. Mix well. Add a little whole wheat bread crumbs or wheat germ to thicken. Form into cutlet. Heat the oil in baking dish. Place cutlets into dish. Bake a little and turn over once. Then bake until light brown. Serves four.

POTATO PUDDING #1

6 potatoes, 1 large Bermuda (or Spanish) onion.

Grate potatoes with skins on and grate onion. Add 1 clove of garlic, minced. Add whole wheat bread crumbs to take up water from potatoes. Bake 30 minutes in hot oven. Sprinkle with parsley when serving and serve with green vegetable salad. Serves three.

POTATO PUDDING #2

1 large Irish potato, 1 large onion, 4 stalks celery, 2 tbs. vegetable oil, 1 large sweet potato, 1 green pepper.

Dice onion, celery, tomato and pepper. Grate or shred potatoes. Mix all together. Place in baking dish and bake until browned. Add oil after removing from fire. Serve hot. Serves two.

POTATO-VEGETABLE PANCAKES

4 large potatoes, 2 carrots, 1 onion, 1/2 lb. squash, 2 tbs. vegetable oil, 2 tbs. vegetable broth powder.

Grate all ingredients on fine grater. Add vegetable broth powder and 1 tbs. vegetable oil. Pour into greased baking dish. Spread rest of oil over top and bake in hot oven for 15 minutes. Then lower flame and bake for 20 minutes more. Serves two.

POTATO-VEGETABLE STEW

2 large Irish potatoes, 1/2 lb. green peas, 1 green pepper, 1/2 head celery, 1/4 bunch parsley, 1 clove pressed or grated garlic.

Dice all ingredients. Half cover with water and steam until tender. Serves four.

BAKED PUMPKIN #1

1/2 small pumpkin, 1/2 lb. raisins.

Cut pumpkin into chunks. Add raisins and sprinkle with lemon juice and honey. Place in oiled dish and bake 20 minutes. May be served with applesauce. Serve with grape juice, if desired. Serves four.

BAKED PUMPKIN #2
1/2 small pumpkin, 4 apples.

Shred pumpkin and apples. Add honey and a sprinkle of cinnamon. Place in oiled baking dish. Bake 25 minutes. Serve with any stew desired or on a vegetable plate. Serves four.

RICE AND VEGETABLE CASSEROLE
3/4 cup brown rice, 1 onion (grated), 1 tsp. vegetable oil, 1 carrot, 1/2 cup precooked peas and celery, 1/2 cup raisins, 2 tbs. honey.

Precook rice for 10 minutes in one glass of water. Put into greased casserole. Add grated carrot, precooked vegetables, raisins, honey and mix. Add 1 1/2 glasses of water and bake for 30–40 minutes. Serves two.

BAKED VEGETABLE SOY DISH
1 lb. soy beans, 2 stalks of celery, 1 tomato, 2 tbs. unsulphured molasses or honey, 2 quarts water, 1 onion, 1 green pepper, 1 clove garlic (if desired), 1 tbs. oil.

Add juice of one lemon to water. Soak beans overnight in water. In summer keep in refrigerator. In morning boil for 2 hours or until tender. Pour off excess water, if any, and save for soup.

Chop two stalks celery, one onion, one green pepper, and cut up tomato or add tomato juice. Add to the mixture and bake in hot oven for 25 minutes. Remove from fire and sprinkle with oil. Add garlic if desired before baking. Serves four.

SQUASH PANCAKES

1 lb. squash, 1/2 lb. parsnips, 1 large onion, 1 large clove of garlic, 1 tbs. oil, whole wheat bread crumbs.

Grate squash, parsnips, onion and garlic. Mix with oil. Form into pancakes and roll in whole wheat bread crumbs. Bake in lightly greased pan in hot oven for 30 minutes. Bake on both sides. Serves four.

STUFFED YELLOW SQUASH (A favorite Florida Spa Recipe)

Scrub squash with stiff brush. Cut off bottom end and scoop out. Chop fine and add diced tomatoes, grated onion, finely minced green pepper, and minced parsley. Add vegetable powder. Steam for a few minutes, then stuff squash with this mixture. Place in oiled baking pan and cover with a little oil. Then bake in medium oven until squash is tender. Serves one.

VEGETABLE CHOP SUEY #1

In another part of this book we are stressing the value of sprouts generally. However, since soybean sprouts enter into the preparation of some of the Chinese dishes, here is a short resume of how to grow them.

a.) Wet an ordinary dish towel in lukewarm water.

b.) Fold towel in thirds—on bottom and middle layer spread one layer of green mung beans evenly.

c.) Place the folded towel and layers of sprouting beans in a large shallow container or platter.

d.) Pour over a small amount of lukewarm water to keep towel and contents continually moist.

e.) Place in a very warm spot, and in about 3 days beans should be sprouted. A wonderful protein and vitamin and mineral rich food.

Can be used raw in a raw vegetable salad and in combination with other vegetables in dishes such as chop suey.

Fresh soy bean sprouts can also be bought at Chinese food stores or Chinese restaurants.

1/2 lb. brown rice, 1 onion, 1 cup diced celery, 1/2

cup tomato juice, 6 ozs. soy sprouts (or 1 small can ready to use obtainable from Chinese stores or better health food stores). Steam brown rice for 30 minutes. Cut up onions and celery. Add tomato juice and soy bean sprouts and simmer for 10–12 minutes. Pour mixture over brown rice. Serves two.

VEGETABLE CHOP SUEY #2

2 cups shredded Chinese cabbage, 3 stalks sliced celery with tops, 2 sliced onions, 1/4 lb. soybean sprouts, 2 cups water, 1 1/2 lbs. corn or potato starch, 1 tbs. vegetable oil, 1 sliced green pepper.

Mix onion and celery and steam for 7 minutes. Add water and starch, and steam for 7 additional minutes. Add rest of ingredients and simmer until tender. Add oil and a little vegetable broth powder. Serve with brown rice. Serves two.

VEGETABLE DELIGHT

2 sweet potatoes, 1/2 lb. tart prunes, 1 bunch small beets.

Scour prunes. Shred beets and potatoes. Pit prunes and cut into small pieces. Add the potatoes and beets. Steam for 25 minutes in 2 cups water. Serve with shredded coconut honey, if desired. Serves four.

VEGETABLE LOAVES

The following recipes of vegetable roasts provide not only good wholesome nourishment, they are enjoyable and satisfying. They can also be served as a fine substitute for any of the protein dishes.

FLORIDA SPA VEGETABLE LOAF

Combine any assortment of cooked vegetables, except beets. Add sauteed onions and dried boiled chestnuts. Have ingredients quite dry. Bake in well oiled casserole. Serve with a vegetable sauce.

GROATS LOAF

1/2 cup coarse buckwheat groats, 1 carrot, 1 onion, 1 stalk celery, 2 glasses water, 2 tsp. vegetable flavoring.

Shake groats in pan over flame until crisp. Add grated carrot, onion, minced celery, flavoring and boiled water. Bake for 30-40 minutes in greased uncovered casserole. Serves two.

VEGETABLE-NUT LOAF

1 cup cooked green peas, 1 cup cooked stringbeans, 1 raw carrot, 1 tsp. vegetable flavoring, a pinch of marjoram, 1 cup ground nuts, 1 onion, 1/2 apple, 1 tbs. wheat germ, a little parsley.

Grate apple, carrot and onion. Grind or chop all other ingredients and add a tbs. of vegetable oil. Mix and pour into greased baking dish. Spread a little oil over top or dot with butter. Bake in medium oven for 30-40 minutes. Serve with tomato sauce, tomato juice or favorite relish. Serves three.

POTATO LOAF

6 potatoes, 2 carrots, 2 onions, a little parsley or vegetable broth powder. Shred all vegetables. Mix well together. Bake in oiled dish until browned. Serve on lettuce leaves. Serves three.

POTATO AND SQUASH LOAF

Grate the following ingredients:
4 potatoes, 1 onion, 1/2 lb. squash, 1 carrot.

Add: 2 tbs. whole wheat flour, 1 tsp. vegetable oil, 2 tbs. vegetable broth powder. Grease dish and bake 25-35 minutes. Serves two.

SWEET POTATO LOAF

2 large sweet potatoes, 1 lb spinach, 2 onions, 1 bunch parsley.

Scrub potatoes thoroughly. Bake for 15 minutes. Grate with the skin. Chop vegetables fine, add to grated sweet potatoes and bake in slow oven in oiled dish for abour 1/2 hour. Serve with relish, if desired. Serves four.

BROWN RICE LOAF

2 cups brown rice, 1 bunch carrots, 1/2 lb. string-beans, 2 onions, 1 bunch celery.

Wash rice and soak overnight in enough water to cover. Grind or grate onion, celery, stringbeans and carrots with skin after scrubbing them thoroughly. Mix with rice and bake 30 minutes in oiled dish. Sprinkle paprika for color and flavor. Serve with favorite relish. Serves ten.

VEGETABLE RICE LOAF

3/4 cup brown rice, 1/2 cup green peas, 3 stalks celery, 1 large carrot, 1 onion, 1 tsp. vegetable flavoring, 2 tbs. vegetable oil.

Steam rice with peas and celery in 1 1/2 glasses of water for 20 minutes. Add grated carrot, chopped onion, flavoring, and 1 glass of water. Add 1 tbs. vegetable oil, mix well, pour into greased baking dish. Pour balance of oil over top of loaf and bake for 30–40 minutes in medium oven or until brown. Oil may be omitted from this recipe. Serves five.

VITAMIN ROAST

1 young cabbage, 1/2 lb. spinach, 1/2 bunch celery, 1 green pepper, 1 onion, 1 cup nut meal or chopped nuts.

Grind vegetables. Add nut meal or chopped nuts and bake in oiled dish. Serve with sauce given below. (Those with delicate digestions should substitute string beans for cabbage). Serves four.

Sauce: 2 onions, 1/4 lb. okra, 2 cups tomato juice, 1 pepper, 3 stalks celery, 1 clove of garlic, 1 tbs. potato flour.

Dice onions, pepper and celery. Mince garlic or slice fine. Put all ingredients in tomato juice and cook on low flame for 15 minutes.

DESSERTS AND PUDDINGS

Desserts should be eaten after a meal only if still hungry. Always remember that the fresh fruits and berries are best.

Here is a list of some of the most enjoyable desserts, including some that are cooked.

BAKED APPLES

4 apples, 1/2 cup seedless raisins.

Core apples, fill with raisins in center. Place in baking dish and add glass of water. Bake for 25 minutes. Serve with honey or molasses if additional sweetening is desired. Serves four.

APPLE-SWEET POTATO DESSERT (A Florida Spa Delicacy)

Slice partially cooked sweet potatoes into 1/4 inch thickness. Place layer in greased pie plate. Place a layer of sliced apples above it. Add a little honey and cover with another layer of sweet potatoes. Bake for about 50 minutes in 350° oven.

BLUEBERRY (OR HUCKLEBERRY) DESSERT

1 box of blueberries or huckleberries.

Wash the berries thoroughly and stew on low flame without adding any water. Takes only a few minutes to stew. Add sliced bananas. Serves three.

SUMMER FRUIT CUP

1/2 peach, 1/2 pear, 1/2 slice pineapple, 1/2 slice watermelon, a few blueberries.

Dice fruit and mix with berries. Add honey and chill before serving. Serves one.

MELON DESSERT

Scoop honeydew and watermelon balls. Add green grapes, blend with a little honey and chill just before serving. Makes a quick colorful dessert.

RICE PUDDING

1 cup brown rice, 2 tbs. honey, 3 cups water, 1/2 cup raisins.

Boil rice in 3 cups of water for 15 minutes. Drain rice. Add raisins and honey. Mix well and bake in greased pan for 20 minutes.

RICE AND APPLE PUDDING

1 cup steamed brown rice, 1/4 cup honey, 2 apples, 1 quart water, 1 cup seedless raisins.

Steam rice in water until tender. Core and shred apples. Mix with rice, raisins and honey. Bake 25 minutes and serve. Sprinkle with wheat germ and berries or shredded coconut. Serves four.

MAKE EATING A SUCCESSFUL VENTURE

When seventy-year-old Bruce O., a Montana rancher, came to consult us about his arthritis problem, he was so enthused about the benefits he had derived from the change we made in his eating habits that he actually started to sing its praises. "Let's not call it a 'diet' when what it really means is changing to a healthful way of living. Once this is understood," he continued, "you begin to realize that it means *no* deprivation or denial." Then he took each letter of the word "diet," and explained that what the arthritis victim has to develop is a "delicious, imaginative, exciting technique" in food preparation. While this involves a choice of the best and healthiest foods, it also presents a challenge to the imagination and ingenuity of the individual to prepare meals that are enjoyable and delightful.

By the time Bruce came to consult us about his arthritis problem he had already undergone a right hip-replacement operation, and while the surgery in his case turned out satisfactorily, the arthritis in many of his other joints caused a great deal of suffering. His left hip, the lower part of his back and both of his shoulders gave him a great deal of pain, he hoped that, by adopting a carefully regulated health program, he would avoid a replacement operation in his left hip, and while accomplishing this, also clear up the arthritis in the rest of his body.

Remember the point that Bruce O. made about "diet" being a *delicious, imaginative, exciting technique of food preparation.* This means choosing the kinds of food that can help you to get well and keep well. By using your imagination and versatility you will find that you can prepare the kinds of meals that are most enjoyable. Work at it: choose the foods that you like best, but also make sure that they are the best foods for you! Remember, you are adopting a healthful way of living because you are determined to get well, and the only way you can get well is by discarding foods that are bad for you and by choosing the kinds of food that provide the nourishment you need.

KITCHEN UTENSILS AND APPLIANCES

The following utensils and appliances are helpful in the preparation of meals:

Vegetable graters or grinders (a Foley food mill or an electric blender). They grate raw vegetables such as carrots, beets, parsnips, turnips, cabbage, cucumbers. Pick those that are easiest to handle. They are of special help for those who, because of their dentures, find chewing difficult, and are also labor saving.

A stainless steel vegetable steamer or pressure cooker. What a difference in the flavor and taste of foods that are steamed or prepared in a pressure cooker!

Whenever possible get a vegetable juicer. Carrot juice,

carrot and celery juice; carrot, celery and apple juice; carrot and cabbage juice—what a variety of other juices that can be combined and are pleasurable as well as beneficial!

A blender can be used to good advantage. It can help you prepare most delectable fruit desserts as well as a variety of other enjoyable food mixtures.

Don't overlook a seed grinder, it works wonders with seeds, nuts and grains, when chewing them is difficult.

And remember the sprouting equipment available in the health food stores, sprouts are a great addition to your meals. You should find the chapter on sprouting most helpful, and what a joy it is to use them as they keep growing!

A FEW SUGGESTIONS

Raw ground cauliflower and zucchini go well in a raw vegetable salad. Also chopped raw spinach. Finely minced parsley and other herbs may be added as seasonings, but make sure that they are freshly dried good quality herbs. Use fresh basil instead of dried, when available (this is easy to grow in a summer garden, or potted on a windowsill). Chopped or diced onions will lose their "bite" if they are immediately soaked in cold water. After draining the water, add fresh lemon juice, it mellows them.

In conclusion we wish to remind you that while this section of the book presents a list of foods that the arthritis sufferer will find most enjoyable, they still must not forget that periodic fasts or liquid diets offer relief of pain and do much to hasten recovery.

ENJOYABLE DISHES FROM PATIENTS' RECIPES

We asked some of our arthritis patients to list some of their own dishes that they have found most enjoyable, and here are some of them:

From Mildred S.'s kitchen, the lady whose story is appearing in Chapter 1.

PINEAPPLE COLE SLAW
    1 cup grated cabbage, 1/2 green pepper chopped

very fine, 2 sprigs parsley-minced, 1/4 cup pineapple freshly grated, or drained crushed pineapple, garlic powder to taste.

Mix first five ingredients. Add meal mixed with pineapple juice and toss. Garnish with a little more dry meal when serving. Serves 1 or 2. Those who have never tried garlic flavor in a slaw are in for a delightful surprise.
Dressing: 2 tbs. almond or sunflower seed meal mixed with a little pineapple juice.

POT LUCK FRUIT AND CABBAGE SALAD
2 cups shredded cabbage, 1 medium apple chopped, 1 small ripe banana cut in small pieces; handful of grapes—halved or quartered, few raisins, 1/2 cup pineapple freshly grated or crushed drained.

Toss all ingredients with dressing. Garnish with a little more dry meal when serving. Serves three. You may omit or add any fruit you have on hand. Almost any fruit goes well in this salad.
Dressing: 2 tbs. almond or sunflower seed meal mixed with a little pineapple juice.

HAPPY DAY FRUITS WITH SWEET POTATO
2 sweet potatoes baked or boiled and skinned, 1 peach stewed, 1 pear stewed, 3 apricots stewed, 1/2 cup cubed pineapple, 1 1/2 tbs. sunflower seed oil, 2 tbs. orange juice, 1/2 tsp. cinnamon or more to taste, honey to taste.

Lightly oil small casserole dish. Slice cooked sweet potato about 1/4 inch thick. Place in casserole. Add sliced stewed peach, pear, pineapple, and halved apricots in layers. Pour over this the oil, orange juice, cinnamon and honey. Mix together. Bake in 350° oven for about 30 minutes. Serves 2 or 3. Garnish with a little crushed coconut or cinnamon when serving.

VARIETY SWEET POTATOES

Bake sweet potatoes at 425° for about 1 hour. Cut in half and scoop out, saving shells. Add any of the following for each potato: 1 tsp. honey, 2 tbs. fruit juice—apple, pineapple or orange. Mash and mix well. Add one chopped pitted prune for each potato and/or a little crushed pineapple. Mix. Fill shells. Return to 350° oven for about 10 minutes. Serve hot.

SWEET RICE DISH—EAST INDIAN STYLE

1 cup brown rice (long grain), 2 1/2 cups water, honey to taste, raisins—handful; coconut—crushed, (about 1/4 cup) or almond meal.

Add rice to water in sauce pan. Bring to boil. Reduce heat to simmer. Add raisins, coconut and almonds (if slivered). Let simmer until all water is absorbed. If almond meal is used, it should not be added until rice is served. Add honey to taste before serving. Sprinkling of cinnamon may be added to enhance flavoring. Serves four.

RECIPES FROM GLADYS C. C.'s KITCHEN

When we asked sixty-plus-year-old Gladys C. C., who for years has been kept on pain-suppressive remedies for her arthritis, also high blood pressure pills, and who is now well on the road to recovery, to write out some of the recipes that she found most enjoyable, she was only too glad to accommodate. Here are some of her recipes:

VITAMIN "C" SALAD

Shred fine lettuce leaves, endive, dandelion greens, romaine, garden cress, beet tops and spinach. Toss well with nut butter dressing sweetened to taste with honey.

CABBAGE, STRING BEAN AND CARROT SALAD

4 cups cabbage shredded, 2 large carrots shredded or

chopped, 1 pt. cooked string beans. Marinate vegetables with 1/2 cup favorite salad dressing.

PEAS OR CARROTS
Put dried parsley or mint leaves in cooking water.

SWEET POTATOES
Scoop out sweet potatoes, mash them and add crushed pineapple to taste to mashed sweet potatoes.

FRENCH DRESSING
1 cup vegetable oil, 1/2 cup lemon juice, 1/2 tsp. paprika.

Beat all ingredients with rotary beater. Keep in covered jar in refrigerator. Shake again to mix before using as it separates.

LEMON OR LIME HONEY DRESSING
1/3 cup of lemon or lime juice, 1/3 cup vegetable oil, 1/2 cup honey, 1 tsp. celery or poppy seeds.

Combine all ingredients. Beat with rotary beater until blended and smooth. Serve over fruit salads.

NUT BUTTER DRESSING
Mix well 1 part lemon juice with 2 parts nut butter made as follows. Run 8 heaping tbs. of nuts through a very fine grinder and work into the consistency of butter with 4 tbs. water or lemon juice. Sweeten with a little honey if desired.

DISHES LANIE J. FOUND MOST ENJOYABLE
Recently when thirty-five year old Lanie J. came to our office seeking help, she told us that at the age of eleven she was already suffering from what doctors called erythema nodosum, an acute inflammatory skin disorder accompanied by tender red nodules with itching and burning. While

growing up she continued to suffer from repeated colds, fever, and other respiratory ills. Twice she developed pneumonia. She also had two operations; first for the removal of her tonsils, later for the removal of her appendix. Last year she was hit by a severe attack of rheumatoid arthritis. Her knees became badly swollen. They were tapped several times and she had pains all over her body. During all this time she had been kept on aspirin.

She stopped taking aspirin from the moment she started with our care, and if you ask her now, just a few months later, how she feels, she'll tell you "Great!" We asked Lanie to write out some of her recipes and here they are:

FRUIT SALAD

Can be made with different combinations of fruit with nuts or seeds sprinkled on top. It's fun to make up new combinations too.

1.) 1/2 cup each of diced fruit: bananas, apples and raisins, top with 1/4 cup chopped walnuts.

2.) 1/2 cup each bananas, pears, seedless grapes, 1/4 cup sliced almonds.

3.) 1/2 cup each bananas, papaya, pineapple, 1/4 cup sunflower seeds.

4.) 1/4 cup each bananas, apples, grapes and cooked yams, 1/4 cup black or white sesame seeds.

A complete lunch served on bed of greens with celery hearts and carrot sticks.

ORIENTAL CHEESE

8 oz. farmer cheese (cottage or pot cheese), 2 tbs. dried "hiziki" seaweed, 1 tbs. green pepper minced, 2 scallions, sliced or chopped, 1/2 cup mung bean sprouts, lightly steamed and chopped, garlic powder, kelp powder, paprika.

Soak "hiziki" in 1 cup hot water about 1/2 hr. (Reserve soaking water.) Drain and mix with cheese. Vegetables can be coarsely chopped in blender and then mixed with cheese. Add garlic powder and kelp powder to taste and mix in 2–4 tbs. seaweed, soaking water to moisten and hold together the mixture. Sprinkle paprika on top. Use as a spread or a dip or for a complete lunch. Serve on a bed of shredded lettuce garnished with radishes, carrots, cucumbers and tomatoes. Serves two.

NEAR EASTERN SALAD

1 cup of couscous (soak 1/4 cup couscous in 1 cup of water overnight—cooking unnecessary), coarsely chopped vegetables (in blender or by hand); 1 stalk celery, 2 scallions, 5 sprigs of parsley (approx.) 1/2 cucumber, 1 medium tomato, olive oil, lemon juice and garlic powder to taste.

Mix couscous and vegetables together. Mixture may be watery, so drain if necessary (save water for soup or drink it). Dress with oil, lemon juice and garlic powder. Complete meal served on lettuce and garnished with avocado slices. Serves one.

Incidentally when we told Lanie that a change to our pattern of living will also have a stabilizing effect on her nervous system, she couldn't at first believe it, but then she was amazed when a few weeks later she noted how much calmer and relaxed she was.

SOME OF SALLY B.'s RECIPES

Sally found her way to us about forty-five years ago when, in addition to her arthritis, she suffered from agonizing headaches. Medicine did not relieve her headaches. She can never forget how our type of care helped her. Here are some of her recipes:

STRING BEANS

Steam with sweet basil in covered saucepan until tender.

OVERCOMING ARTHRITIS ◆ 218

EGGPLANT

Peel and slice eggplant, steam until tender, place in greased pyrex pan. Add tomato slices, season with onion powder and oregano, and then place cheese slices on top (goat's cheese) and bake in hot oven until crust forms.

CUCUMBER SALAD

Slice cucumber, marinate with lemon juice, olive oil, onion powder and fresh chopped parsley or dill.

BEET SALAD

Steam beets with skin on, then peel and slice and marinate with lemon juice, oil, onion powder, kimmel or cloves in powder form.

LENTIL STEW

Wash one cup lentils in strainer. Place in saucepan and add four cups of water, cover tightly and simmer until half done. Then add 1/2 cup cubed celery, one carrot cut up, half a green pepper, an onion. When cooked, grate in one clove of garlic. Cook on very low flame.

POTATO SOUP

Simmer slowly diced celery, carrot, green pepper, parsnip and parsley root for ten minutes. Add four potatoes diced, and simmer ten or fifteen minutes on low flame. When done, add parsley and dill chopped very fine. Makes delicious soup.

EGGPLANT STEW

Peel and slice one eggplant, one carrot, add 1/2 cup diced celery, half green pepper and one onion. Place in saucepan on low flame and cover tightly. Simmer slowly for about 30 minutes. When done, add one clove of grated garlic.

TRUDY R.'s RECIPES

Then comes Trudy who wishes to share some of her recipes with us. When Trudy came to us about thirty or more years ago she was full of arthritis. But now about thirty or more years later, she doesn't mention anything about the disease. She is still attractive, and looks younger than when she first came to us and besides getting well, she has learned how to stay well for life. Here are some of her recipes:

EASY POTATO CHIPS

Lightly oil large baking dish. Thinly slice well-scrubbed potatoes (white or sweet). Place in single layer on dish. Bake till brown and puffed.

STUFFED ARTICHOKES

4 large or 6 small artichokes

Cut off bottom outer artichoke leaves if brown and part of stem. Remove choke in center of artichoke. Toast about 5 slices whole wheat bread. Dice—add small clove crushed garlic, handful chopped fresh parsley, little oregano and little olive oil. Mix together and stuff center of artichokes. Place in 1" to 1 1/2" of water. Cook till tender about 45 minutes to 1 hour (or 15 min. in a pressure cooker). Serve with large salad.

AUNT RAY's LIMA BEAN SOUP

Cook baby limas (1 lb.) in about 2 qts. water for approx. 1 hour. Add small turnip diced, 4 carrots diced, 3 large onions diced, several stalks celery diced, handful fresh peas, handful string beans diced. Tie up handful fresh dill and parsley. Cook till vegetables are tender. Add Hain's vegetable seasoning.

Optional: May add 1/4 cup barley along with limas. May add small diced potato to vegetables. May add bay leaf.

BAKED BROCCOLI AND CHEESE

Steam broccoli till fairly tender. Place on lightly oiled baking dish, sprinkle about 1 tbs. saf or soy oil over top. Sprinkle little garlic powder, Hain's vegetable seasoning and little oregano over top. Place layer of cottage cheese on top. Bake uncovered until cheese is melted.

LAYERED EGGPLANT OR ZUCCHINI

Lightly oil baking dish. Thinly slice and peel eggplant or slice zucchini. Put thinly sliced onions over, then add thinly sliced peppers, then sliced tomatoes.

On top of vegetables add thinly sliced goat cheese or ricotta cheese. Repeat as from beginning. Top with cheese. Cover. Bake in fairly hot oven for 45 minutes. Uncover, bake another 10–15 minutes.

TASTY RICE

Cook brown rice as directed. Sauté celery (several stalks), onions and green peppers. Add a little soy sauce, a few shakes of garlic powder, and a little ground vegetable seasoning. Add rice. Mix thoroughly and serve.

MILLET AND BANANA

Cook millet as directed. Add thinly sliced or mashed banana. Heat together. Little honey optional.